T0323708

Cambridge Elements ☰

Elements in Second Language Acquisition
edited by
Alessandro Benati
The University of Hong Kong
John W. Schwieter
Wilfrid Laurier University, Ontario

THINKING AND SPEAKING IN A SECOND LANGUAGE

Yi Wang
Cardiff University
Li Wei
University College London

CAMBRIDGE
UNIVERSITY PRESS

CAMBRIDGE
UNIVERSITY PRESS

University Printing House, Cambridge CB2 8BS, United Kingdom

One Liberty Plaza, 20th Floor, New York, NY 10006, USA

477 Williamstown Road, Port Melbourne, VIC 3207, Australia

314–321, 3rd Floor, Plot 3, Splendor Forum, Jasola District Centre, New Delhi – 110025, India

103 Penang Road, #05–06/07, Visioncrest Commercial, Singapore 238467

Cambridge University Press is part of the University of Cambridge.

It furthers the University's mission by disseminating knowledge in the pursuit of education, learning, and research at the highest international levels of excellence.

www.cambridge.org
Information on this title: www.cambridge.org/9781009074841
DOI: 10.1017/9781009075053

First published 2022

A catalogue record for this publication is available from the British Library.

ISBN 978-1-009-07484-1 Paperback
ISSN 2517-7974 (online)
ISSN 2517-7966 (print)

Thinking and Speaking in a Second Language

Elements in Second Language Acquisition

DOI: 10.1017/9781009075053
First published online: May 2022

Yi Wang
Cardiff University

Li Wei
University College London

Author for correspondence: Yi Wang, WangY471@cardiff.ac.uk

Abstract: Does the language we speak affect the way we think? This Element provides a synthesis of contemporary research on the interplay between language and cognition in speakers of two or more languages and examines variables deemed to impact bilingual acquisition and conceptualization of language-specific thinking patterns during L2 learning. An overview of different yet interrelated studies is offered across a variety of conceptual domains to illustrate different approaches and key variables. The comparison of monolingual and bilingual data demonstrates the highly integrative nature between L2 learning and the changing of one's entire cognitive outlook in L2 speakers. This Element makes relevant connections between language learning and bilingual cognition, aiming to shed new light on how learners acquire conceptual distinctions of the target language(s). It also raises theoretical and pedagogical issues that encourage teachers to reflect upon how to incorporate recent advances in language-and-cognition research with aspects of L2 teaching.

Keywords: linguistic relativity, second language acquisition, bilingual cognition, teaching pedagogy

ISBNs: 9781009074841 (PB), 9781009075053 (OC)
ISSNs: 2517-7974 (online), 2517-7966 (print)

Contents

1 What Are the Key Concepts?

The question of whether the language we speak shapes the way we think has generated extensive debate in recent decades. The study of how language influences thought, also known as linguistic relativity (Whorf, 1956), has recently received renewed interest as a number of new research paradigms have evolved that allow addressing the interplay between language and thought empirically.

Experimental evidence suggests that cross-linguistic differences in linguistic encoding can 'augment certain types of thinking' (Wolff & Holmes, 2011, p. 253), such as attention, recognition memory, visual discrimination, sorting and categorization, in a flexible and context-dependent manner. For instance, cross-linguistic differences in colour vocabularies can cause differences in colour categorization, indicating that language effects are profound in the sense of affecting even basic 'categorical perception' (i.e., faster or more accurate discrimination of stimuli that straddle a category boundary, Regier & Kay, 2009, p. 439). However, such linguistic relativity effects are vulnerable to short-term manipulations, such as recent linguistic priming (Montero-Melis et al., 2016), the language of instruction (Athanasopoulos, Bylund et al., 2015) and verbal interference (Gennari et al., 2002).

Given the great complexities of language-and-thought research, in Section 1, we introduce a number of key terms and concepts surrounding the notion of the language–thought interface. Specifically, we are going to discuss what thought is, where we can find it and in what form it is manifested. We will then go over current views of when and where language effects on thought are most likely to arise. This helps to sketch out the cognitive mechanisms at play for linguistic relativity effects and paves the way for further discussions of the language-and-thought interface in speakers of more than one language.

1.1 What Is the Language-and-Thought Interface?

The theoretical basis of the language-and-thought interface is grounded in one of the most extensively debated theories, namely the linguistic relativity hypothesis (LRH), also known as the Sapir–Whorf hypothesis (Whorf, 1956). The LRH postulates that language and thought are interrelated, and people who speak different languages embody different world views depending on the linguistic categories made available in those languages. For example, when expressing the duration of time, speakers of Swedish and English, who prefer distance-based metaphors and describe time as 'long' and 'short' (Alverson, 1994; Evans, 2004), represent the passing of time differently compared to speakers of Greek and Spanish, who prefer amount-based metaphors and describe time as 'big' and 'small' (Casasanto et al., 2004; Lakoff & Johnson, 1980).

While the idea that language is related to thought extends a long way back to the early days of Western philosophy (see Lucy, 1997, 2016, for a historical review) – for instance, von Humboldt viewed language and thought as an inseparable unit with each language giving its speakers a particular 'worldview' (von Humboldt, 1963, p. 60) – this issue gained its most prominence via the work of Edward Sapir and Benjamin Lee Whorf. In Whorf's words,

> We cut nature up, organize it into **concepts**, and ascribe significances as we do, largely because we are parties to an agreement to organize it in this way-an agreement that holds throughout our speech community and is codified in the patterns of our language. [...] We are thus introduced to a new principle of relativity, which holds that all observers are not led by the same physical evidence to the same picture of the universe, unless their linguistic backgrounds are similar, or can in some way be calibrated. (Whorf, 1940, pp. 213–214)

The basic tenet of the LRH is that languages 'carve up' the world in different ways. Thus, if the language people speak constrains them to attend to the external world in certain ways, speakers of different languages will develop distinct views and concepts of the reality in ways that reflect language-specific properties.

> The linguistic relativity principle ... means ... that users of **markedly different grammars** are pointed by **their grammars** toward different types of observations and different evaluations of externally similar acts of observation, and hence are not equivalent as observers but must arrive at somewhat **different views of the world**. (Whorf, 1940/1956, p. 221)

To be more specific, Whorf (1956, p.158) clearly explains each notion and puts emphasis on the effects of 'grammars' and 'different views of the world'. By 'grammars', Whorf means habitual lexical and grammatical patterns of a language, such as 'lexical, morphological, syntactic, and otherwise systemically diverse means coordinated in a certain frame of consistency'. 'Different views of the world', on the other hand, is typically understood as 'thought' or 'concepts' that modulate speakers' habitual or routinized ways of conceptualizing, perceiving and classifying reality.

Following Lucy (1992a, 1992b), the definitions of 'concepts' and 'thought' in present-day psycholinguistic research are typically operationalized as a wide array of non-linguistic (or non-verbal) behaviours and mental processes, including attention, reasoning, perception recognition memory, problem-solving, sorting and categorization. These processes are non-verbal in nature because they do not involve or elicit overt language comprehension or production, but manifest certain forms of cognitive or perceptual responses to given stimuli (Athanasopoulos & Bylund, 2020; Bylund & Athanasopoulos, 2014b; Casasanto, 2008; Gallistel, 1989). This line of reasoning also resonates with Pavlenko's (2005, p. 435) definition of concepts, which refers to 'mental representations that affect individuals' immediate perception, attention, and recall and allow members of specific language and culture groups to conduct identification, comprehension, inferencing and categorization along similar lines'.

1.1.1 Does Language Determine Thought?

Since its formulation, the LRH has taken various forms (for an evaluation of different models, see Wolff & Holmes, 2011). A strong view of it is known as linguistic determinism, which holds that language shapes or determines thought (Brown & Lenneberg, 1954). According to Brown and Lenneberg (1954), 'languages are moulds into which infant minds are poured' (p. 454). This language-as-mould metaphor, as pointed out by Casasanto (2008, 2016), has two major flaws. First, language does not necessarily shape thought permanently or at only one point in time (i.e., early childhood) during one's entire cognitive development. Second, language is not the sole shaper of thought. In line with Casasanto's influential argument, Wolff and Holmes (2011) also remind us that although language triggers thought, thinking is possible without language. In this view, linguistic determinism overexaggerates the shaping role that language has. In fact, research from the cognitive sciences has indicated that the relationship between thought and the world is much tighter than that between thought and language, with plenty of evidence showing that differences between languages are much more diverse than differences observed in people's mental representations (Casasanto, 2016; Lucy, 1992a, 1992b; Munnich, Landau, & Dosher, 2001; Regier & Kay, 2009; Roberson, 2005; Wolff & Malt, 2010).

Despite having been hotly debated for more than half a century, language determinism has difficulty in holding ground as no empirical evidence has ever been found to support this radical claim. In contrast, an increasing amount of research has illustrated that linguistic relativity effects, rather than rigidly shape one's world view, tend to mediate or affect aspects of cognition in a flexible and context-dependent manner (Casasanto, 2008; Levinson, 2001; Trueswell & Papafragou, 2010; Wolff & Holmes, 2011). For example, in the domain of colour, recent studies show that cross-linguistic differences in colour naming affect the discrimination of colour (Athanasopoulos et al., 2010; Regier & Kay, 2009; Roberson, 2005; Thierry et al., 2009; Winawer et al., 2007). For instance,

Winawer et al. (2007) reported that obligatory colour distinctions in Russian between *golouboy* (light blue) and *siniy* (dark blue) affected one's processing speed in colour discrimination. Speakers of Russian, who have two basic lexical items for blue (*golouboy/siniy*), responded much faster when matching two colours belonging to different categories (i.e., one is golouboy and the other is siniy) than within the same category (i.e., both are bolouboy or siniy). However, such patterns were not observed in speakers of English, who only have one basic lexical item for blue. In a similar vein, Thierry et al. (2009) examined how colour category boundaries affect categorical perceptions of colour in Greek and English speakers using event-related potential (ERP) techniques. It was found that speakers of both Greek and English were perceptually aware of the distinctions between two shades of blue and green, as indicated by their brain activation patterns. But Greek speakers, who have two basic colour items for light and dark blue (i.e., *ghalazio* and *ble*), but only one basic item for light and dark green (i.e., *prasino*), displayed greater brain activation for blue than for green contrasts, thus showing that language categories affect colour discrimination performance.

On the other hand, turning to the domain of motion, which refers to 'a situation containing movement of an entity or maintenance of an entity at a stationary location' (Talmy, 1985, p. 60), Papafragou et al. (2002) reported that although speakers of English (satellite-framed language) and Greek (verb-framed language) differed significantly in how motion is talked about (i.e., English: a man walking across the street; Greek: a man crossing the street (walking)), their categorical preferences for manner and path were far more similar than their naming patterns.

In summary, the overall findings suggest that the effect of language on cognition is not a simple 'yes-or-no' question. The fundamental issue here is to discover what aspects of language tend to affect what dimensions of thinking and in what ways (Bylund & Athanasopoulos, 2014b; Casasanto, 2016).

1.1.2 What Are the Main Controversies?

Over the years, the LRH has sparked much controversy in the disciplines of Linguistics, Psychology, Philosophy and Anthropology (for critical discussions, see Casasanto, 2008, 2016; Lucy, 1997, 2016; Pinker, 1994). On the one hand, criticism on of the LRH partly comes from the strong version of linguistic determinism, since it oversimplifies the intricate connection between language and cognition. As pointed out by Pavlenko (2011, p.19), interpreting the LRH as a simple 'yes-or-no dichotomy' is a misinterpretation of Whorf's original concepts. In fact, the determinism view is a later invention introduced by those who attempted to reformulate the ideas but lost their original arguments in translation (Pavlenko, 2011, 2016).

On the other hand, at the opposite extreme is the 'universalist' position, in which thought is said to be free, universal and entirely independent of language (Pinker, 1994; see Casasanto, 2008; Thierry, 2016, for further discussions and critical evaluation). Being the best-known criticism of linguistic relativity, the rationale behind this approach is the Universal Grammar (Chomsky, 1975), which claims that human cognitive behaviours are guided by universal perceptual biases and not subject to language-specific properties. Although language-specific properties can reflect some facets of our cognitive functions, they neither mould nor guide thought (1975, p. 4). Pinker further suggests that 'language is not necessary for concept acquisition nor does it "pervade[e]" thought' (Pinker, 1994, p. 17). Under this view, the notion that 'differences among languages cause differences in the thoughts of their speakers' is 'wrong, all wrong' (Pinker, 1994, p. 57).

The universalist approach has triggered numerous debates concerning the link between language and the rest of the mind. In a later explanation, Pinker (1994) proposes that 'the idea that thought is the same as language is an example of what can be called a conventional absurdity [.]' (p. 57). However, as highlighted by Casasanto (2008), most of the critiques from the universalist camp centre around the so-called Orwellian claim that 'the idea that thought is the same as language' (Orwell, 1949), rather than the Whorfian effect (i.e., whether language shapes thought). As a result, rejecting the language as language-of-thought assumption does not mean that we are ready to accept the opposite view and consider language–thought interdependence as an alternative option.

In fact, several groundbreaking studies from cognitive neuroscience and brain neurophysiology have challenged the universal dominance of human cognition and view language as an essential and indispensable part of the human mind (Athanasopoulous et al., 2010; Boutonnet et al., 2013; Thierry et al., 2009). This perspective is well reflected in Thierry (2016), who further suggests that it is misleading and essentially meaningless to separate language from the rest of cognitive general abilities, and 'thinking that language may be entirely disconnected from thought is an example of what deserves to be called *reductio* ad *absurdum*' (p. 691). To sum up, the main controversies regarding linguistic relativity effects are situated at two extremes of a conceptual continuum. While we do not find support for these two opposing views, there is converging evidence that language can affect cognition via numerous mechanisms (see Wolff & Holmes, 2011, for an overview). We will focus on different mechanisms via which language affects cognition in the following sections.

1.1.3 Contemporary Approaches to Language-and-Thought Research

As noted earlier, neither the universalist view nor a strong view of linguistic determinism can successfully unravel the mechanism underlying the relationship between language and thought. With the development of multidisciplinary research in the twentieth century, the LRH received renewed interest after the dominance of the universal-based approach. Contemporary approaches to language–thought research (also known as the 'neo-Whorfian' approach) adopt a multidisciplinary perspective and emphasize the need to implement both linguistic and non-linguistic paradigms when addressing the language-and-thought debate (Bylund & Athanasopoulos, 2014b; Levinson, 2003; Lucy, 1997, 2014, 2016; Majid et al., 2004). For instance, contemporary researchers have begun to place psycholinguistic methods at the centre of testing and try to operationalize the Whorfian question using modern cognitive theories that precisely characterize the nature and complexity of cognitive effects (Lucy, 1992a, 1992b; Lupyan, 2012; Slobin, 1996). Furthermore, recent advances in the fields of neurophysiology and the cognitive neurosciences have provided researchers with new opportunities to discover the neural correlates of language effects on cognition, thus providing more nuanced evidence for the complexities involved in language and cognitive processing (see Athanasopoulos & Casaponsa, 2020, for a recent review).

To be more specific, by directly utilizing a variety of behavioural measures, such as triad-matching, recognition memory, attention allocation, as well as reaction times (Levinson, 2001, 2003; Lucy & Gaskins, 2001, 2003; Papafragou et al., 2008; Regier & Kay, 2009; Roberson & Davidoff, 2000), together with neurophysiological techniques, such as eye-tracking, ERPs and functional MRI (Athanasopoulos et al., 2010; Boutonnet et al., 2013; Flecken et al., 2015a; Thierry et al., 2009), the interface between language and attention has been examined in a wide array of cognitive domains. For instance, findings from the domain of colour suggest that speakers with different word labels for colours are found to be more efficient in colour recognition (Franklin et al., 2008; Gilbert et al., 2006; Regier & Kay, 2009; Roberson et al., 2008; Thierry et al., 2009; Winawer et al., 2007). Cross-linguistic differences across languages have also been observed in how people think about objects and substances (Ameel et al., 2005; Imai & Gentner, 1997; Pavlenko & Malt, 2011), as well as more abstract conceptual categories such as time (Boroditsky et al., 2011; Boroditsky et al., 2003; Casasanto & Boroditsky, 2008), number (Athanasopoulos, 2006; Cook et al., 2006; Lucy, 1992a; Lucy & Gaskins, 2001, 2003), gender (Bassetti & Nicoladis, 2016; Bender et al., 2018; Sato & Athanasopoulos, 2018), spatial frames of reference (Levinson, 2001, 2003; von Stutterheim et al., 2017) and motion events (Flecken et al., 2015a; Gennari et al., 2002; Montero-Melis & Bylund, 2017; Trueswell & Papafragou, 2010).

The prevailing question 'Does the language we speak influence the way we think?' can then be replaced by a battery of more specific investigations, such as when and where are the language effects on cognition mostly likely to appear? What is the exact cognitive mechanism that gives rise to such effects? And how can we most precisely uncover the nature of such effects? The answers to these questions will provide us with more precise definitions of aspects of language and cognition and advance our understanding of the role of language within cognition.

1.2 Thinking for Speaking: Where Is It?

The notion of thinking-for-speaking (TFS) was proposed by the psycholinguist Dan I. Slobin (1987, 1996, 2000, 2003) as an influential version of the LRH (Casasanto, 2015), arguing that the activity of thinking takes on a particular quality when it is employed in the activity of speaking (Slobin, 1996, p. 76). Specifically, when Slobin talks about 'thinking for speaking', he focuses on the effect of language on thinking that is conducted during the processes of speaking, writing, translating or remembering. From this perspective, thinking is 'a special form of thought that is mobilised for communication' (Slobin, 1996, p. 6) and its effect is limited to online processes only.

More specifically, TFS postulates that language channels one's attention. When people are involved in language-induced activities, such as comprehension or speech production, they need to pick those elements that (1) fit some conceptualization of the event and (2) are readily encodable in language (Slobin,1987, p. 435). As a consequence, the linguistic constraints of different languages may guide speakers to attend to specific details of information when talking about them. The crucial difference between the LRH and TFS, therefore, is that the former emphasizes the language effects on habitual thought regardless of whether language is being in use or not, while the latter focuses on thinking patterns during active language use.

According to Slobin (1991)one way to investigate 'thinking for speaking' is by focusing on a child's first language acquisition. When children acquire a native language, they might learn particular ways of thinking (p. 2). Research along these lines is interested in exploring whether child speakers of different languages exhibit language-specific thinking patterns and when during the course of L1 development TFS effects start to appear (Allen et al., 2007; Berman & Slobin, 1994; Choi & Bowerman, 1991). Another way to gain insights into 'thinking for speaking' is by looking at L2 learners, concentrating on the questions of (1) whether language patterns acquired in childhood are 'resistant to restructuring in adult second language acquisition' (Slobin, 1996, p. 89), and (2) what difficulties learners may encounter during the acquisition of thinking patterns associated with the L2.

The TFS hypothesis has mainly been investigated in the motion domain, starting with observations of speakers' speech and gesture patterns. In terms of expressions of motion, one influential framework within this line of research is based upon Talmy's (1985, 2000) typological distinctions between so-called satellite- and verb-framed languages. For example, when expressing the mundane event 'A boy walks up a hill', speakers of satellite-framed languages (S-languages) such as English and German, encode the manner of motion ('walk') in the main verb, whereas manner-of-motion information can be omitted in other languages. Talmy's typological framework has turned out to be particularly useful in cross-linguistic comparisons across the world's most spoken languages. By using a wide range of speech elicitation methods (i.e., spontaneous speech and narrative production), studies examining the speech and gestures of children and adult speakers of various languages (Duncan, 2001; Hickmann & Hendriks, 2006, 2010; Hickmann et al., 2009; Kita & Özyürek, 2003; McNeill, 1997, 2000; Montero-Melis & Bylund, 2017; Özyürek et al., 2005) have reported apparent cross-linguistic differences in how speakers think, speak and gesture about motion.

While substantial evidence suggests that speakers of different languages select and organize information in language-specific ways (Berman & Slobin, 1994; Slobin, 2003, 2006; von Stutterheim et al., 2017; von Stutterheim & Nüse, 2003), recent studies have questioned whether differences between languages can be equated with differences in thought processes (Athanasopoulos & Albright, 2016; Casasanto, 2008, 2016; Lucy, 2014, 2016). As pointed out by many scholars, using linguistic data alone may run the risk of circular reasoning (i.e., language-on-language effect), since the only evidence that people who talk differently also think differently is that they talk differently (Casasanto 2008, p. 67). To gain a better understanding of the cognitive implications of language-specific features in human thinking processes, an increasing number of studies within the TFS paradigm have started to combine speech production with a variety of dynamic measures to capture the mental processes concurrent with verbal production.

These methods include experimental paradigms using multimodal tasks, such as attention, recognition memory and categorization, often coupled with co-verbal behaviours that involve gestures (Brown & Gullberg, 2008; Cadierno, 2008; Stam, 2015), eye movements (Flecken et al., 2014; von Stutterheim et al., 2012), reaction times (Ji & Hohenstein, 2018; Wang & Li, 2021b) and ERPs

(Athanasopoulos et al., 2010; Flecken et al., 2015a). For example, using an eye-tracking paradigm, Papafragou et al. (2008) explored how Greek and English speakers directed their visual attention to different components of motion events (i.e., manner and path of motion) in the process of speech preparation. Results showed that compared with English speakers, Greek speakers were more likely to prioritize their attention to path over manner when preparing for speech. However, such language-specific effects subsequently disappeared when participants simply watched the motion scenes freely. In a similar vein, von Stutterheim et al. (2012) explored how the presence and absence of grammatical aspect in the target language influence the extent to which speakers attend to different components (i.e., the goal or the ongoing phase) of motion events. Grammatical aspect is a linguistic category that denotes the internal temporal property of a situation (Comrie, 1976; Dahl, 2000). For example, in English, grammatical aspect is systematically encoded on the main verb, and there is an obligatory distinction between the ongoing (i.e., A man is crossing the street, imperfective/progressive aspect) and the completed (i.e., A man has crossed the street, perfective aspect). However, in other languages, such as German and Swedish, there is no such grammatical device to convey this contrast.

Combining language production with attention allocation and recognition memory, von Stutterheim et al. (2012) reported that speakers of languages that provide obligatory grammatical means to convey aspectual contrasts, or aspect languages (i.e., English, Arabic and Spanish) tended to mention end points less frequently compared with speakers of languages that lack obligatory grammatical means to denote such contrasts, or non-aspect languages (i.e., German, Dutch and Czech). At the same time, speakers of aspect languages directed less attention to end points and stored less information about them in their working memory. In addition, visual attention patterns provided a more nuanced picture, that is, speakers of aspect languages also looked at event end points at a later point than speakers whose languages do not contain such grammatical device during speech planning. The findings thus indicate that looking at co-verbal behaviour such as visual attention provides us with a unique window into real-time processing in the preparation of describing an unfolding event (Athanasopoulos & Casaponsa, 2020).

Using ERP techniques, Flecken et al. (2015a) studied the influence of grammatical aspect on the perceptual processes of event construal in speakers of English and German. As noted earlier, speakers whose languages have grammatical aspect (i.e., English) are more likely to attend to the ongoing phase of an event (i.e., A man is walking along a street) than speakers whose languages lack the progressive aspect (i.e., German) (von Stutterheim et al., 2012). In the experiment, participants were asked to perform a matching task with their ERPs being recorded. In each trial, participants watched a one-second animated prime showing basic motion events, in which a dot travelled along a trajectory (curved or straight) towards an end point of a geometrical shape (square or hexagon). But the end point was never reached. Then participants were engaged in a picture matching task in which the target animation was followed by a picture symbolizing event end points or trajectories in four different conditions: a full-match condition (5 per cent) where both end point and trajectory matched the target (i.e., a dot moving along a curved trajectory towards a square), a full-mismatch condition (75 per cent) (i.e., a dot moving along a straight trajectory towards a hexagon), an end point match condition (10 per cent) (i.e., a straight line) and a trajectory match condition (10 per cent) (i.e., a hexagon). Participants were instructed to respond only to the full-match condition. Results showed that speakers of German displayed larger P3 amplitude (an ERP component used for reflecting conscious processes involved in attentional processing) in end point match conditions than in trajectory match conditions, while English speakers did not display any differences. The authors therefore concluded that cross-linguistic differences in grammatical properties affected lower-level processing, and speakers of different languages automatically allocated their attention to the linguistic elements highlighted by grammar.

Using a triad-matching paradigm, Gennari and colleagues (2002) took the first step within the TFS paradigm and investigated whether cross-linguistic diversities in linguistic encoding moved beyond verbal behaviour and affected English (S-language) and Spanish (V-language) speakers' recognition of and categorical preferences for manner and path. Speakers of English and Spanish were allocated to one of three conditions: a 'naming first' condition, during which participants described all motion videos prior to recognition and similarity judgements; a 'free' condition where participants watched motion in silence; and a 'shadow condition' in which participants were instructed to repeat aloud nonword syllables while watching the videos. Results showed that while shadowing led to an overall decrease in path-congruent selections in both English and Spanish, only Spanish speakers selected significantly more path-congruent choices after the 'naming first condition' compared with the 'shadow condition'. In a more recent study, Wang and Li (2021b) coupled the triad-matching paradigm with reaction times and extended the domain of interest to early Cantonese–English bilinguals whose language pairs do not exhibit contrastive typological differences. In the 'naming first' condition, the bilinguals were randomly allocated to either a Cantonese- or English-speaking condition during which they had to verbalize all motion videos in the target language prior to similarity judgements. In the 'shadowing condition', participants had to repeat numbers while making categorical judgements. This study showed that both bilinguals' categorical preferences and reaction times exhibited language-specific patterns in the naming condition. However, when speakers' access to language was blocked in the shadowing condition, the impact of language on cognition could only be found in the implicit measurement of reaction times. The findings suggest that combining the triad-matching paradigm with reaction times can better capture the automatic and implicit processes during one's decision-making, thus providing new insights into one's entire cognitive profile.

To conclude, there is consistent evidence showing that speakers of different languages think differently in processes where language is being covertly or overtly used. However, less consensus has been reached in conditions where one's access to language is hindered (i.e., conditions with verbal interference). Thus, it would be interesting for future studies to compare findings for this shared phenomenon and approach the interface between language and thought from different angles in different disciplines.

1.3 How Do Language-on-Thought Effects Arise and What Is the Underlying Mechanism?

In light of the observations discussed earlier, there has been increasing consensus on the sophistication of language effects on cognition and on the multiple factors involved in determining when and where such underlying effects are more likely to appear (Lucy, 2016; Lupyan, 2012, 2016; Thierry, 2016).

Recent advances in the language-and-though debate have suggested that effects of language on non-linguistic representations depend on a wide array of factors, such as the involvement of language in non-verbal tasks, the nature of the stimuli and different cognitive domains under investigation (see Bylund & Athanasopoulos, 2014b; Lucy, 2016 for detailed reviews). For instance, relativity effects are more prominent in circumstances where language is utilized for online thinking or as an aid to complete subsequent cognitive tasks (Bylund & Athanasopoulos, 2014b; Slobin, 1996, 2003). However, some relativity effects may weaken or even disappear when one's access to language is minimized, suppressed or blocked by a concurrent verbal interference (Athanasopoulos, Bylund et al., 2015; Dolscheid et al., 2013; Gilbert et al., 2006; Trueswell & Papafragou, 2010; Winawer et al., 2007).

Given that language affects aspects of cognition to various degrees across contexts, a possible way of understanding the likely mechanism that underlies the interaction between language and cognition is the label-feedback hypothesis proposed by Lupyan (2012), which is concerned with the role of linguistic labels in category formation and perceptual representations. According to

Lupyan (2012), language plays a paramount role in category formation. For example, hearing the name of a 'dog' activates language-specific labels/representations of the 'dog' category in a bottom-up fashion. Meanwhile, diagnostic features associated with the category being labelled (i.e., dog) become warped in a top-down manner. The practice of labelling and its associated perceptual features are frequently co-activated via a phonological loop, which can be flexibly up- or down-regulated by recent language experience. On the one hand, overt verbal training or linguistic prompts would up-regulate the impact of verbal labels on cognition as speakers could draw on corresponding labels when making their decisions. A context with verbal interference, in contrast, would down-regulate the mutual feedback between linguistic and non-linguistic representations and disrupt the phonological loop and, as a result, the impact that language has on cognition is greatly diminished.

As discussed earlier, we come back to the fundamental question of how relativistic effects arise in cognitive tasks that involve different degrees of language involvement. Using a training paradigm, English speakers in Athanasopoulos and Albright (2016) were asked to categorize novel events based on the degree of goal orientation. As noted earlier, English has grammatical means to specify event phases and speakers of English typically take an immediate perspective and focus more on the ongoingness and initial phase of an event (i.e., two women walking along the road). In contrast, German does not contain grammatical means to indicate the progressive aspect, and as a consequence, German speakers typically adopt a holistic perspective and focus more on the end points of the same event (i.e., two women reaching the house and going inside). In the experiment, participants were allocated to two conditions and provided with constant feedback on their choices. In an English-biased condition, a low–end point clip was correct, whereas in a German-biased condition, the correct answer was a high-end point clip. As expected, in silent categorization, English speakers were more successful in learning low-end point patterns, as they are promoted in their native language. However, in a non-verbal condition with a concurrent verbal interference, learning was only affected in the English-biased condition, not the German one. The rationale behind this was that, in a silent condition, speakers could covertly draw on verbal processes to complete the task. However, when English verbal interference was introduced, the recruitment of verbal labels was disrupted. As grammatical aspect habitually encoded in English was not the criterion for high-end point decisions, speakers' categorical preferences in a German-biased condition were thus not affected. The authors concluded, therefore, that categorization is verbally mediated, and the verbal interference can selectively enhance or mute the use of prior knowledge in cognition.

In a similar vein, Vanek (2020) went one step further and examined the strength of language-induced facilitation in cognitive processing by controlling for different degrees of language involvement. Using a perceptual learning paradigm, Chinese learners of L2 English were trained to categorize change-of-state events as either goal-oriented (Chinese-like) or action-oriented (English-like) in three conditions: a verbal-explicit condition where access to L2 was granted, a silent condition where verbalization was optional and a verbal interference condition where access to L2 was blocked. Results revealed that language had a gradient effect on cognition: categorization with explicit L2 labelling demonstrated the greatest effect, followed by a silent condition and categorization with verbal interference had the least effect. The results indicate that the degree of top-down language influence during task performance can be modulated by manipulating the presence or absence of verbal cues, thus providing new insights into the mechanism behind the effects of linguistic labels in cognitive processing.

The impact of verbal labels on cognition receives further support from behavioural and neural evidence for low-level cognitive processes (Athanasopoulos et al., 2010; Boutonnet et al., 2013; Pan & Jared, 2021; Sato & Athanasopoulos, 2018; Sato et al., 2020). In one such study, Sato et al. (2020) explored how grammatical gender affects attentional biases and categorization of objects in English monolinguals and French–English bilinguals using neurophysiological techniques. Grammatical gender can be found in some languages such as Spanish and German, whereby nouns are assigned either a feminine or a masculine gender category. English, in contrast, does not incorporate such grammatical features. In this study, participants were instructed to make similarity judgements on image sets consisting of gender-associated objects while their brain potentials were recorded. Overall, the findings suggest that grammatical gender modulated attention and categorization basis. That is, French–English bilinguals showed greater N1 and N300 amplitudes in gender-incongruent trials than in gender-congruent trials, indicating that grammatical gender structured attentional basis even in the early stages of the visual processing stream. Also, the effect of gender congruency persisted and continued to shape higher-level processing in a late N300 time window. In light of the above findings, it is suggested that language modulates attention in a top-down manner, and such modulation can occur within as little as 45–85 ms and can continue to shape higher-level processing and categorical judgements in later stages of semantic categorization. In summary, the findings lend support to assumptions that cognitive processing is language-induced and provide convincing evidence for the top-down influence of grammatical structures on sustained attention and semantic integration.

1.4 Conclusion

To conclude, this section takes a multidisciplinary perspective and integrates different theoretical constructs and methodological approaches used for determining the mechanism of the underlying impact of language on cognition. It is concluded that rather than viewing Whorfian effects as 'all-or-nothing' phenomena, current research aims to paint a more fine-grained picture of when and under what conditions language-specific categories interact with general cognitive processes. Based on the latest advances in language and cognition research, it is important to extend the domain of interest to bilingual and second language acquisition (SLA), in order to gain a better understanding of how the interaction between language and cognition is influenced by distinct sets of structures and grammars in individuals who speak two or more languages.

2 What Are the Main Branches of Research?

Section 2 provides a focused overview of research considering the dynamics between multiple languages and sets of concepts in one mind and variables deemed to impact the acquisition and internalization of language-specific cognitive patterns during L2 learning. To be more specific, this section reviews and analyses three theoretical perspectives used to account for L2 speakers' unique patterns of thinking, seeing and gesturing for speaking. The theoretical approaches reviewed here are the multicompetence account (Cook & Li, 2016), the CTH (Jarvis & Pavlenko, 2008) and theories of attentional and associative learning (Smith & Samuelson, 2006). These approaches are unified in nature and aim to delineate why language learning brings about conceptual changes in the individual mind. This section will have implications for future studies to paint a fuller picture of a complex phenomenon, that is, bilingualism, and its interaction with cognition.

2.1 Language and Bilingual Cognition: The Effect of Language Learning on Cognitive Restructuring in the Bilingual Mind

Linguistic relativity research in the past decade has witnessed a shift from the traditional focus on monolinguals to bilinguals or L2 speakers of two or more languages (Cook, 2003; Cook et al., 2006; Lucy, 2016). Extending language-and-thought research into the domain of bilingualism and L2 learning is deemed to be a natural extension of the LRH, as bilinguals and L2 users are direct practitioners of the relativistic effects (Bylund & Athanasopoulos, 2014b).

Then what does it mean by a second language (L2)? In theory, a second language (L2) refers to any language(s) that is acquired after the first language. However, in practice, the learning profile of L2 speakers is far more complex and diverse. For example, a second language can be acquired early on and in conjunction with the development of the first language. On the other side, L2 learning only starts after the primary development and establishment of the first language. In addition, in the case of children living in a multilingual environment with exposure to two or more languages simultaneously after birth, they may have two or more L1s and L2s given their complicated learning repertoire. In this regard, the term 'L2' or 'additional language' should be taken to reflect more of an analytical abstraction rather than a 'black-and-white' reality (Ortega, 2014, p. 5).

Given the great diversities in bilingual and SLA, the current volume does not qualitatively differentiate bilingual speakers from L2 learners but instead takes various individual factors, including age of acquisition, language dominance, language proficiency, language status (majority vs minority language), contexts for language learning (instructed vs naturalistic), language of schooling (especially for early bilinguals) as well as length of immersion into account when exploring individual learner's unique language learning trajectories.

Research on thinking and speaking in L2 learning is increasingly gaining currency in SLA and bilingual cognition research and this overwhelming trend has been well illustrated by recent volumes and special issues with a variety of empirical and theoretical studies on how the world is represented in speakers of two or more languages (Bassetti & Filipović, 2021; Cook, 2015 Cook & Bassetti, 2011; Han & Cadierno, 2010; Jarvis & Pavlenko, 2008; Pavlenko, 2014). The fundamental questions at the centre of bilingual language-and-thought research are:

- Do bilinguals with different languages think differently from monolinguals?
- Does learning another language change the way people partition reality?
- How do different languages reconcile with each other in the same mind?

These questions are closely related to mental representations of concepts in the bilingual mind, the learnability of L2-based thought patterns and the permeability of already established ways of thinking associated with the L1. Thus, extending relativity research to the contexts of bilingualism and SLA will not only advance our understanding of the dynamics between language and thought, but also provide unique insights into language learning.

Having outlined the major areas of interest in bilingual cognition research, this section reviews three theoretical perspectives adopted in language-and-thought research and summarizes relevant studies that bridge bilingualism and linguistic relativity research. The three main perspectives reflected in the current volume are the multicompetence account (Cook, 1991, 1992, 2002, 2003; Cook & Li, 2016), the CTH (Jarvis, 2007; Jarvis & Pavlenko, 2008;

Pavlenko, 2011) and theories of attentional and associative learning (Samuelson, 2002; Smith, 2010; Smith & Samuelson, 2006). These approaches aim to explain why additional language learning brings about conceptual changes in the individual mind and what factors modulate an individual's cognitive behaviour during L2 learning. It is worth mentioning that it is difficult to capture the malleable nature of bilingual behaviour within a single theoretical framework; therefore, different frameworks need to be combined to address the complex issue of language learning and bilingual cognition.

2.2 The Multicompetence Framework

Multicompetence refers to the knowledge of two or more languages in one mind, or as Cook originally puts it, 'the compound state of a mind with two grammars' (Cook, 1991, p. 112). The concept of multicompetence resonates with Grosjean's seminal article that '[t]he bilingual is NOT the sum of two complete or incomplete monolinguals; rather, he or she has a unique and specific linguistic configuration' (Grosjean, 1989, p. 6).

The basic tenet of multicompetence postulates that all languages in a single mind are interconnected to each other. Under this view, the integration continuum model does therefore propose that different languages in a speaker's mind are on a continuum from total separation to integration, depending on the level of language activation or inhibition in specific communicative settings (i.e., the language mode, Grosjean, 1989). Thus, such a scheme can capture the unique characteristics and variations in individual language users and 'allow us to theorize the interaction between multiple languages in the speaker's mind as a natural and ongoing process and to understand why multilinguals may perform differently from monolinguals in all of their languages, including the L1' (Jarvis & Pavlenko 2008, p. 17).

While multicompetence research starts with cross-linguistic influence phenomena in the areas of formal linguistic features, such as words and structures, a recent wave of bilingualism research has extended the scope of this framework to cover the whole landscape of the L2 user's mind, including wider cognitive processes and concepts, rather than languages alone (Cook, 2016). In a pioneering book entitled *Language and Bilingual Cognition*, Cook and Bassetti (2011) investigated the effects of language learning on bilingual cognition by adopting a multicompetence perspective and raised many intriguing questions: (1) how the learning of multiple languages affects cognition and (2) how to explain the complex phenomenon of bilingualism and its relationship to cognition.

The successful application of the multicompetence framework in bilingual cognition research is based upon the premise that representations in the bilingual mind are highly interactive and multimodal (see Athanasopoulos, 2016, for a review). In this instance, cross-linguistic effects could arise not only in language but also in cognitive systems. Crucial questions are therefore whether the acquisition of an L2 brings about a new way of thinking and, in that case, how L2 users deal with conceptual differences between two different languages and create new ways of thinking pertaining to their L2. When studying the effects of L2 learning on cognition within the multicompetence framework, this line of enquiry puts emphasis on the uniqueness of L2 users and treats them as independent, multicompetent speakers with unique linguistic and cognitive capacities (Pavlenko, 2016). According to Cook (2002, 2003), bilinguals are seen as 'unique combinations' with different uses for language from those of monolingual speakers. A notable yet unique feature of bilinguals is their ability to choose the proper language to use in accordance with the interlocutor type and the level of formality of linguistic and social contexts of interactions (Cook, 2003). For instance, in situations where only one language can be used, bilinguals need to constantly manage cross-activation between two competing language systems and control production in one language (Abutalebi & Green, 2008; Thierry & Wu, 2007). The fact that bilinguals have to 'control attention to the target system in the context of an activated and competing system is the single feature that makes bilingual speech production most different from that of monolinguals' (Bialystok, 2009, p. 3). This premise allows us to shift from regarding monolinguals or native speakers as the 'social norm' and provides a ready platform for discovering the cognitive architectures and characteristics that bilinguals have rather than deficiencies compared with monolingual L1 speakers (Cook 2003, p. 5).

Research on the effects of language learning on cognition within the multi-competence perspective started with studies on object categorization and number cognition (Athanasopoulos, 2007; Cook et al., 2006), and it has been successfully incorporated into different research paradigms (Han & Cadierno 2010; Pavlenko 2011). As a pioneering study, Cook et al. (2006) examined whether grammatical number affected Japanese–English bilinguals' categorization preferences for objects and substances. Syntactically speaking, English is a noun class language that uses inflectional morphology to distinguish count nouns (e.g., one apple or three apples) and mass nouns (e.g., water-waters [the form of 'waters' is ungrammatical]), whereas Japanese is a classifier language that lacks such count-mass distinction. Consequently, when performing a similarity judgement task, speakers of English tended to base their judgements on shape, while speakers of Japanese tended to base their decisions on material properties (Imai & Gentner, 1997; Lucy, 1992a). For bilingual speakers, results showed that Japanese learners of L2 English tended to group objects based on their shape, exhibiting an English-like way, and the degree of conceptual changes was modulated by the length of stay in an L2-speaking environment. Along the same lines, Athanasopoulos (2006) extended the findings of Cook et al. (2006) on how number was cognitively represented in the bilingual mind to Japanese learners of L2 English with varying degrees of L2 proficiency. Given the cross-linguistic differences between English (a plural-marking language) and Japanese (a non-plural-marking language) in terms of number marking, results suggested that advanced L2 speakers patterned with English in being more sensitive to number differences between countable and noncountable objects, while speakers with intermediate L2 proficiency behaved more similarly to their Japanese counterparts. Overall results show that L2 users draw on conceptual categories from both of their languages while making their decisions and the degrees of separation and integration of language-specific concepts depend on various individual and contextual factors.

2.3 The Conceptual Transfer Hypothesis

Another closely related strand in bilingual language-and-thought research has been framed by the CTH (Jarvis, 2007, 2011; Jarvis & Pavlenko, 2008; Pavlenko, 2011). In traditional cross-linguistic research, 'language transfer' or 'cross-linguistic influence' refers to interactions between two languages. Odlin (1989) defines language transfer as 'resulting from the similarities and differences between the target language and any other language that has been previously (and imperfectly) acquired' (p. 27). Based upon the observation that cross-linguistic influence takes place not only at formal linguistic levels (i.e., phonological, morphological, syntactical and semantic) but also at conceptual levels (Jarvis, 2007, 2011), Jarvis (2007) refers to conceptual transfer as 'certain instance of cross-linguistic influence in a person's use of one language originates from the conceptual knowledge and patterns of thought that the person has acquired from another language' (p. 44). For example, the notions of 'privacy' and 'personal space' are lexically encoded in English but not in Russian (Pavlenko, 2002a, 2002b, 2003). It is found that cross-linguistic differences in lexical encoding may affect speakers' use and interpretation of these concepts (Pavlenko, 2003). For instance, in a verbal recall task, English monolinguals and Russian–English bilinguals observed certain situations as 'invasions of personal spaces' (e.g., a man sitting too close to a woman), while monolingual Russians did not draw on these notions. In addition, Russian–English bilinguals frequently appealed to lexical borrowing and loan translation from English when expressing this concept in Russian narratives, even though this may lead to ungrammatical L1 constructions. From this perspective, conceptual transfer is interested in examining the interaction between the transfer of language structures and the development of concepts and 'focuses more on the effects of cognition on language use – particularly the effects of patterns of cognition acquired through one language on the receptive or productive use of another language' (Jarvis, 2011, p. 3)).

2.3.1 What Are the Concepts?

Conceptual transfer is grounded in theories of cognitive linguistics and concerns the effects of word meanings and grammatical constructions on the expression and mental representation of concepts (or vice versa) (Jarvis, 2007, 2011). Then what does concept mean? According to Goldstone and Kersten (2003), concept means 'a mentally possessed idea or notion' (p. 600). Given its psychological foundation, Jarvis (2011) defines concept as 'a mental representation of an object, quality, action, event, relationship, situation, sensation, or any other perceivable or imaginable phenomenon for which the mind creates a mental category' (p. 4). In a similar vein, Pavlenko (2005) refers to concepts as 'mental representations that affect individuals' immediate perception, attention, and recall and allow members of specific language and culture groups to conduct identification, comprehension, inferencing and categorization along similar lines' (p. 435).

According to Jarvis (2011), concepts consist of a knowledge component that allows speakers to judge whether objects belong to the same group and categorize them based on their common features. Concepts are also subject to constant changes as one's life experience and social practices change over time. In this view, conceptual transfer can help to explain how grammatical and structural differences between the first and second language could bring about cross-linguistic influence in conceptual and mental processes related to language (Jarvis & Pavlenko, 2008). From this perspective, it aligns with the definition from Odlin, who regards conceptual transfer as 'those cases of linguistic relativity involving, most typically, a second language' (Odlin, 2005, p. 5).

On the other hand, conceptual transfer covers not only concepts but also a dynamic process of conceptualization. Conceptualization, as von Stutterheim and Nuse (2003) puts it, refers to 'a process of forming temporary mental representations of complex situations and events and is used to account for language-specific patterns of thinking during language production' (p. 256). It is also referred to as the preverbal stage in Level's (1989) speech production model, which involves picking up the selected linguistic elements that fit the situation (i.e., macroplanning) and organizing them in accordance with linguistic frames or references (i.e., microplanning). In this regard, conceptualization transfer is more concerned with how conceptual differences in one language affect the use of another language, such as comprehension, speech preparation or production. For example, Daller et al. (2011) found evidence for conceptualization transfer in Turkish–German bilinguals' linguistic encoding of motion events. Using a storytelling task, this study showed that bilinguals transferred most of the language-specific conceptualization patterns (i.e., the use of path verbs) from the more-dominant language to the less-dominant language in speech production. The authors concluded that the findings constitute clear evidence for the linguistic manifestation of how motion events have been conceptualized in the individual mind.

As discussed earlier, the fundamental questions here are about what is being transferred, and how deep it runs. According to Jarvis (2007), conceptual transfer refers to effects arising from cross-linguistic differences in structures or concepts stored in the mind of L2 users, while conceptualization transfer comes from cross-linguistic differences in how L2 users select and organize concepts to reflect a particular event and form temporary representations at the moment of language use. Studies anchored in the former typically use a wide array of non-verbal tasks, such as perception (Athanasopoulos, 2009; Flecken, 2011), recognition memory (Filipović, 2021; Koster & Cadierno, 2019) and categorization (Bylund & Jarvis, 2011; Park & Ziegler, 2014), while the latter focuses on verbal processes such as speech production (Brown & Gullberg, 2011; von Stutterheim & Carroll, 2006; von Stutterheim & Nuse, 2003), comprehension (Chamorro et al., 2016; Liu, 2018) and object naming (Ameel et al., 2005; Pavlenko & Malt, 2011). It is worth mentioning that while it is of theoretical value to distinguish between conceptual and conceptualization transfer, it is not always possible or necessary in practice to differentiate these two and pin down the exact source of transfer (Jarvis, 2007, 2011).

2.3.2 What Is the Relationship between Conceptual Transfer and Linguistic Relativity Research?

According to the CTH, speakers of different languages embody distinct sets of concepts and representations of reality. In the case of bilinguals and L2 users, conceptual differences acquired in one language may affect how another language is learnt and used. Within this framework, the interface between language and cognition has triggered a number of important questions, including (1) the extent to which bilinguals are able to restructure their conceptual representations of reality towards the target language; (2) the interaction between linguistic and non-linguistic representations in the bilingual mind and (3) linguistic or extra-linguistic factors that can mediate the process of restructuring during L2 learning (Bylund & Athanasopoulos, 2014b; Wang & Li, 2021a).

In this regard, the CTH seems to be a natural extension of the linguistic relativity principle as both approaches are closely associated with cross-linguistic differences in conceptual meaning. In a relevant study, Bylund and Jarvis (2011) explored conceptualization differences related to grammatical aspect in bilinguals of Spanish (with grammatical aspect) and Swedish (without grammatical aspect). Using a video description task and a grammaticality judgement test, it was found that Spanish–Swedish bilinguals mentioned end points more often compared with Spanish monolinguals and showed less sensitivity to aspectual errors in the grammaticality judgement, thus indicating a backward transfer of L2-based conceptualization patterns to the L1. This study suggests that conceptual transfer differs from linguistic reality in a number of important ways. First, the CTH assumes that cross-linguistic differences in conceptual meaning only appear in language use (e.g., the speech planning process). In this regard, the scope of conceptual transfer overlaps to a large extent with TFS (Jarvis, 2016). Second, the CTH assumes that language specificity in lexical and grammatical constructions is not the only source for all the differences in mental concepts. It also allows the potential impact of extra-linguistic biological or sociocultural factors on bilingual cognition. From this perspective, the scope of conceptual transfer only partly overlaps with the linguistic relativity principle and should be viewed as a bridge that links traditional cross-linguistic influence research and linguistic relativity research (Jarvis, 2016). When it comes to the CTH, it is therefore important to take both verbal and non-verbal evidence into account to better illustrate when conceptual transfer occurs, in which conceptual domain, and how it impacts bilinguals' interpretation and expression of conceptual meaning. This also provides new insights into the nature of conceptual or conceptualization transfer, such as what it consists of, how deep it runs and how it correlates with aspects of general cognition.

2.3.3 What Are Different Forms of Conceptual Changes?

Taking multicompetence into account, conceptual transfer is dynamic and multi-directional in nature whereby an L1-based concept can affect and be affected by L2-based concepts. For example, in terms of directionality, conceptual transfer can take place in either a forward (L1→L2) or backward direction (L2→L1). In this regard, conceptual transfer seems to be more inherently bidirectional and convergent than other types of transfer (i.e., structural or semantic transfer) (Jarvis & Pavlenko, 2008). For example, studies examining the conceptualization pattern of motion events suggest that bilinguals or L2 users show simultaneous influences from both languages and their performance falls in-between monolingual baselines (e.g., Brown & Gullberg, 2008; Hohenstein et al., 2006). The interconnection between concepts gives rise to different degrees of transfer in the bilingual mind and, therefore, conceptual changes are graded and exhibit various forms. Based on Pavlenko's (1999, 2000) approach to concepts in bilingual memory, Jarvis and Pavlenko (2008) outlined five stages of conceptual changes from an analytical perspective as reviewed later in this Element. It is worth mentioning that cognitive restructuring is a dynamic and ongoing process where each stage occurs either simultaneously or developmentally without an absolute fixed order.

Internalization of New Concepts

Cognitive restructuring starts with the internalization of novel categories, perspectives or reference frames absent in the L1. It is also legitimate to talk about the internalization of new categories, perspectives, frames and/or patterns of preference that result in target-like performance (Pavlenko, 2011, p. 247). One typical example comes from the domain of grammatical gender, that is, learning a new language that has grammatical gender may bring about new ways of assigning gender to inanimate objects in speakers whose native language lacks a grammatical gender system (Boroditsky et al., 2003; Kurinski & Sera, 2011).

Convergence

Convergence is viewed as a particular kind of restructuring that may involve 'L1 and L2 values, distinctions, or boundaries' (Pavlenko, 2004, p. 52). In this process, speakers may exhibit a unitary conceptual category incorporating constructions from both L1 and L2 and display an 'in-between performance' (Pavlenko, 2011, p. 247). As an example, Park (2020) found that bilinguals of Korean (verb framed) and English (satellite framed) performed differently from their monolingual counterparts in motion event categorization: bilinguals selected more manner-based choices than Korean monolinguals, but fewer manner choices than English monolinguals, thus indicating an 'in-between' performance between two monolingual baselines.

Conceptual Shift

In order to reduce the cognitive load of keeping different sets of concepts, speakers are prone to shift from their L1-based concepts, but reassembling, albeit not necessarily fully, to L2-based concepts (Pavlenko, 2011, p. 247). For instance, English speakers typically categorize objects based on common shape, while Yucatec (Lucy, 1992a) or Japanese (Imai & Gentner,

1997) speakers tend to categorize objects based on common substances or materials. It was found that Yucatec or Japanese learners of English altered their categorical preferences from shape to material as a function of L2 proficiency, thus indicating a conceptual shift towards the L2-based category.

Restructuring

Prolonged experience with the L2 may also result in another type of conceptual change, namely, the restructuring of L1-based concepts or L2 influence on L1 categories, involves 'a partial modification of already existing language-mediated conceptual categories' (Jarvis & Pavlenko, 2008, p. 160). Consequently, conceptual restructuring results in 'some changes or substitutions, or a partial shift' (Pavlenko, 2000, p. 179). L2 influence on L1 is a gradual process and can be found in bilinguals' linguistic and non-linguistic behaviours. Unlike the aforementioned conceptual changes, this process serves as an instance of reverse influence (i.e., L2→L1) in terms of directionality.

Conceptual Attrition

Conceptual attrition is defined as the loss of some L1 elements 'seen in [the] inability to produce, perceive, or recognise particular rules, lexical item, concepts, or categorical distinctions' (Pavlenko, 2004, p. 47) and 'at times accompanied by substitution' (Jarvis & Pavlenko, 2008, p. 169) under the impact of another competing language. As an example, Pavlenko (2002a) found that Russian–English bilinguals with many years of residence in the United States no longer drew on the Russian-based emotion category *'perezhiva'* (suffer things through) when expressing sorrow compared to Russian monolinguals. It is worth noticing that the effect of cross-linguistic influence such as borrowing, convergence, restructuring or loss of previously acquired elements may be permanent, which occurs not only in bilinguals' verbal behaviours (i.e., production) but also non-verbal behaviours (i.e., perception and comprehension) (Jarvis & Pavlenko, 2008; Pavlenko, 2004).

2.4 Mechanisms beyond Cognitive Restructuring: A User-Based Approach to Associative Learning

Researchers in bilingualism and SLA have been interested in blending different methods and approaches as ways to assess how L2 acquisition affects cognition. In order to work out the mechanism that underlies how language learning gives rise to relativistic effects in speakers with more than one language, another strand related to bilingual cognition research is a usage-based approach, namely, the associative and attentional learning account (ALA) (Samuelson, 2002; Smith, 2010; Smith & Samuelson, 2006).

The psychological ALA is concerned with early noun learning in children's L1 development, and its original underpinning is that word learning entails the acquisition of associations between word forms and properties that words refer to. In order to successfully establish instances of form-meaning associations and figure out their statistical probability of occurrence in different contexts, learners need to rely on a variety of semiotic resources made available to them, be they visual, textual, graphical or auditory and among others. For example, children show systematic attentional bias to different properties of objects, such as the shapes of objects, the materials of substances or the colours of the foods, depending on relevant linguistic and context cues (Booth & Waxman, 2002; Imai & Gentner, 1997; Yoshida & Smith, 2001, 2003). For instance, children tend to show a shape bias towards a novel category when it occupies the object position of a verb such as *break* or *make,* in the context of entities with angular and solid properties (i.e., make a muffin). On the contrary, children tend to show a material bias when the novel category occupies the object position of a verb such as *squish, eat* and *spill,* in the context of entities with rounded, flat and irregular properties (i.e., eat some muffins) (Smith & Samuelson, 2006). The ALA claims to be very powerful in delineating the process of attentional learning, because '(a) it is exquisitely tied to and integrates multiple (perceptual and linguistic) contextual cues in the moment; (b) it enables the learner to attend to the same perceptual object in different ways depending on context (e.g., "a muffin" cues attention to shape but "some muffin" cues attention to material) and (c) attention and learning in the moment are strongly guided by the history of regularities in the learner's past' (Smith & Samuelson, 2006, p. 1340).

Based on the observation that representations are integrative, dynamic and highly intercorrelated across modalities (Athanasopoulos et al., 2015; Casasanto, 2016; Kersten et al., 2010; Lupyan, 2012), Bylund and Athanasopoulos (2014b) took the initiative in incorporating the associative learning account with bilingual language-and-thought research to uncover the nature of the language effects on cognitive behaviour. The starting point for linking cognitive restructuring to associative learning is that representations in the bilingual mind are dynamic and interconnected. For instance, neuroscientific evidence shows that the processing of colour labels co-activates with the expected language area, as well as areas in the visual cortex associated with vision (Athanasopoulos et al., 2010; Lupyan, 2012; Regier & Kay, 2009; Thierry et al., 2009). Language-specific representations are built up, or emerge, in an up-regulated fashion (Lupyan, 2012; Smith & Samuelson, 2006). The practice of labelling and its associated representations are frequently co-activated via a phonological loop, which can be flexibly up- or down-regulated by recent language experience. Then, linguistic relativity effects arise, as a consequence of the frequently occurring associations between linguistic and non-linguistic patterns. Regularities in categorization emerge and become part of one's cognitive routine depending on the degree of exposure to specific associations. From an L2 learning perspective, because we are continuously exposed to novel form-meaning associations throughout our lifetime, the fundamental question lies in how L2-specific associations develop over time and what factors tend to modulate this process (Athanasopoulos, Damjanovic et al., 2015; Bylund & Athanasopoulos, 2015; Vanek, 2020).

As pointed out by Bylund and Athanasopoulos (2014b), cognitive restructuring can be interpreted in terms of three major claims for associative and attentional learning. First, associations between form-meaning mappings are highly context-dependent and speakers can attend to the same object in different ways based on the specific context. In such a study, Athanasopoulos and Albright (2016) trained English speakers to categorize novel events based on different criteria (i.e., end point- or ongoingness bias). Using a perceptual learning paradigm, this study showed that English speakers exhibited different categorization patterns depending on contextual cues. The findings thus indicate that contexts play a paramount role in organizing and forming new conceptual categories.

Second, according to the account of associative and attentional learning, similarities that characterize any category are statistical, rather than absolute and sufficient (Smith & Samuelson, 2006). For example, in the process of language learning, learners need to figure out the statistical regularity of a structure and the contexts in which it is most likely to appear. For example, in the domain of objects, Lucy and Gaskins (2001, 2003) took a developmental perspective and investigated when during development relativity effects arose. Using a wide array of similarity judgement tasks and materials, results suggested that for stable objects, seven-year olds of English- and Yucatec-speaking children displayed an identical bias towards shape-based choices. However, at the age of nine, English-speaking children remained shape biased, while Yucatec-speaking children shifted to material-biased classification. For malleable objects, where English and Yucatec exhibited similar grammatical structures, both seven-year olds and nine-year olds showed an overall preference for material-biased choices. The authors, therefore, concluded that cross-linguistic differences from one language to another are a matter of relative degree, rather than absolute.

Finally, perception and categorization are regulated by the history of regularities in the speaker's learning experience. In a seminal study, Athanasopoulos,

Damjanovic et al. (2015) successfully anchored the associative learning approach in explaining the mechanism behind the effects of grammatical aspect on thought. In the motion domain, the availability of grammatical aspect affects the degree to which speakers direct their attention to different components of a certain event (i.e., event trajectories or end points) (Athanasopoulos & Albright, 2016; Flecken et al., 2015a; von Stutterheim et al., 2012). For instance, speakers of languages that have grammatical means to convey aspect-ual meanings (i.e., English) tend to express end points less frequently and focus more on the ongoingness of the target event, while speakers of languages that do not contain grammatical means to denote aspect (i.e., German) show a linguistic bias towards end points more frequently and allocate more attention to action goals. Using a triad-matching task, this study showed that English learners of L2 German biased their choices on event end points, rather than ongoingness, and this pattern was modulated by the increasing L2 exposure and general L2 proficiency. The authors concluded that as speakers are continuously exposed to new form-meaning mappings throughout their lifetime, the already estab-lished associations are open to constant changes as a function of individual learner's development trajectories.

2.5 Conclusion

In sum, this section has summarized three core theoretical perspectives that have been adopted in bilingual cognition research. These perspectives address the interactions between language and cognition in the multicompe-tent mind with separate yet related constructs, which inform us about differ-ent aspects of bilingual cognition. By combining different theoretical frameworks, models and approaches, the dialogue between language learn-ing, bilingualism, and cognition will bring together views and perspectives from various disciplines and will become increasingly important both meth-odologically and theoretically in order to facilitate our understanding of the mechanisms underlying language learning and the malleability of the bilin-gual mind.

3 What Are the Key Readings?

This section takes a more extensive look at current research examining the effect of language learning on bilingual cognition within the aforementioned theoretical approaches. In the first part, we approach this issue by systematically reviewing a substantial number of relevant studies across different conceptual domains and in different modalities (i.e., verbal, co-verbal and non-verbal modalities), anchoring them to the theoretical frameworks discussed earlier.

In the second part, we offer an in-depth discussion of the multiple factors involved in the restructuring process and interpret how these factors function and interact with each other in predicting bilingual cognition.

3.1 The Effects of Language Learning on Bilingual Cognition

3.1.1 L1 Influence on L2

Let us start with the effect of one's first language on a second one, known as L1 transfer. In this stage, speakers tend to continue relying on their L1-based patterns for speaking, seeing and thinking where no restructuring is evident. Empirical evidence of L1 influence comes from various domains, such as colour (Ervin, 1961; Ervin-Tripp, 2011), objects and substances (Athanasopoulos, 2006, 2007; Cook et al., 2006), space (Levinson, 2003), grammatical gender (Bassetti, 2007, 2011; Boroditsky et al., 2003; Boutonnet et al., 2012; Kurinski et al., 2016; Nicoladis & Foursha-Stevenson, 2012; Sato & Athanasopoulos, 2018; Sato et al., 2020), time (Boroditsky, 2001; Gu et al., 2017; Miles et al., 2011), event series (Tang, Vanek & Roberts, 2021; Vanek & Selinker, 2017) and motion (Brown & Gullberg, 2008, 2010; Carroll et al., 2012; Finkbeiner et al., 2002; Flecken et al., 2015a; Pavlenko & Volynsky, 2015; von Stutterheim & Nuse, 2003), in speech production, co-speech gestures, visual attention, working memory and categorization.

L1 influence has been well documented in the linguistic expression of the manner and path of motion events (see Filipović & Ibarretxe-Antuñano, 2015, for a review), which takes structural difference as a point of departure. Studies to date have reported that the typological differences between S- and V-languages may cause difficulties for learners to 're-think for speaking' about motion events in an L2. For instance, speakers of V-languages (e.g., Spanish, French) learning S-languages (e.g., English, German) tend to mention manner less frequently because manner is often omitted in their L1 descriptions (Cadierno, 2010; Daller et al., 2011; Hohenstein et al., 2006). In contrast, speakers of S-languages learning V-languages may encounter difficulties in expressing motion verbs in a target-like manner, particularly when the description of items involves expressing the crossing of a spatial boundary (Cadierno & Ruiz, 2006; Hendriks & Hickmann, 2015; Larrañaga et al., 2012; Treffers-Daller & Tidball, 2015). For example, Cadierno and Ruiz (2006) reported that Danish (S-language) learners of Spanish (V-language) tended to use manner verbs when describing L2 boundary-crossing events (i.e., the dog ran into the house). However, such constructions are generally avoided by V-language speakers in conditions that contain a categorical change of location (i.e., the dog entered the house (running)) (Aske, 1989; Slobin & Hoiting, 1994).

Apart from speech, the influence of L1-based patterns of TFS comes from speech-associated gestures (Cadierno, 2008; Gullberg, 2009, 2011; Kellerman & van Hoof, 2003; Negueruela et al., 2004; Özçalışkan, 2016; Stam, 2006, 2010). For instance, Kellerman and van Hoof (2003) and Negueruela et al. (2004) examined how Spanish learners of L2 English talked and gestured about path of motion in the L2. As previously mentioned, speech-accompanying gestures exhibit language-specific features (see Stam, 2010 for a review). For instance, when gesturing about motion, Spanish speakers tend to synchronize path gestures with the main verb and have separate gestures for boundary-crossing events, whereas English speakers tend to synchronize path gestures with the satellite and accumulate path gestures in a single clause (McNeill, 2005; McNeill & Duncan, 2000). The studies found that although advanced L2 groups produced fluent and target-like speech at the linguistic level, their accompanying gesture behaviour revealed L1-based thinking patterns. For example, when describing the same scene 'El perro se cae al suelo/the dog fell into the floor' in Spanish and English, respectively, Spanish learners of L2 English continued to synchronize their gestures on the main verb (i.e., *se cae/* fell) rather than the satellite (i.e., *al suelo*/into the floor) in both of their languages. Kellerman and van Hoof (2003) used the term 'manual accents' to capture this disassociation between speech production and gestural behaviour, thus indicating the importance of looking at gestures in second language research, as it provides rich and multidimensional data, often adding more details to what is invisible in speech.

Moving beyond speech and gestures, evidence of L1 influence has also been observed in a variety of non-verbal perception, categorization, working memory and recognition tasks (Boroditsky, 2001; Boutonnet et al., 2012;; Filipović, 2018; Miles et al., 2011; Tang, Vanek & Roberts, 2021;). Cross-linguistic studies on temporal relations suggest that people of different languages have different ways to spatialize time (Bylund & Athanasopoulos, 2017; Casasanto, 2016; Fuhrman et al., 2011). For instance, Boroditsky (2001) examined the conceptualization of spatial metaphors for time in Chinese–English bilinguals. Time in English is frequently conveyed along a horizontal axis (e.g., before, after) and speakers of English use horizontal metaphors to map the future as 'ahead' while the past is 'behind'. In contrast, in Chinese, time is prototypically expressed on a vertical axis (e.g., above, below) and Chinese speakers use vertical metaphors to conceptualize time as 'above' (i.e., 上周/above week, last week) and 'below' (下周/below week, next week). In a semantic comprehension task, participants first saw primes in either a vertical (two balls arranged vertically) or horizontal (two balls arranged horizontally) spatial relation, and were then instructed to judge the truth value of temporal relations in a following statement (e.g., March comes earlier than April) as quickly and accurately as possible. The study found that late Mandarin–English bilinguals, compared with early bilinguals, responded faster to vertical primes and were more likely to draw on vertical cues (L1 based) to think about time even when they were 'thinking for English'. The results suggest that habitual use of vertical expressions in how to talk about time has an impact on how speakers think about time in cognition, and these language-specific spatial-time associations are resistant to restructuring in late L2 learners.

To paint a more nuanced picture of the different stages involved in cognitive processing, Boutonnet et al. (2012) took a neuroscientific approach and examined how grammatical gender affected the categorical judgement of objects in Spanish–English bilinguals by employing picture-sorting tasks with ERP techniques. As stated above, Spanish has a binary gender system and Spanish speakers assign either a 'masculine' or a 'feminine' gender to everyday objects. In contrast, English does not incorporate such grammatical features. In a non-verbal categorization task, the Spanish–English bilinguals and English monolinguals were presented with three object images in an all-in-English environment and asked to make similarity judgements as to whether the third object (i.e., carrot) belonged to the same semantic category as the first two objects (i.e., tomato and celery). The grammatical gender of the objects was manipulated and hidden from the participants. Behavioural data showed that while no differences were found in terms of semantic relatedness and gender consistency, participants' brain wave patterns from ERPs revealed an automated activation of gender information in the process of categorization. The results suggest that bilinguals spontaneously and unconsciously access L1-based gender concepts, although their semantic categorization demonstrates an L2-based pattern. Follow-up studies by Sato and Athanasopoulos (2018) and Sato et al. (2020) provide further evidence about French–English bilinguals' reliance on prior linguistic and conceptual knowledge during both explicit and implicit perceptual judgements, showing a robust effect of L1 on the process of L2 acquisition.

In the studies discussed earlier, L1 influence seems to play a role, either overtly or covertly, in various conceptual domains and across different modalities, especially in the early and intermediate stages of L2 acquisition.

3.1.2 The Interaction between L1- and L2-based Concepts

With increasing levels of bilingual experience, L2 users may start to destabilize originally established thinking patterns and internalize new ones corresponding to the target language (Jarvis & Pavlenko, 2008). For example, grammatical gender (i.e., masculine vs feminine) is a typical grammatical feature in some languages such as Spanish and German (i.e., a key is masculine in Spanish but feminine in German), but not for others (i.e., English and Russian). For example, all nouns in English are assigned with biological gender (i.e., s/he). Recent studies have found that learning a language with grammatical gender can bring about new ways to categorize inanimate objects in speakers whose L1 does not contain grammatical gender categories (see Bassetti & Nicoladis, 2016, for a recent review). In fact, a wealth of recent studies has provided evidence for the internalization of L2-based concepts in different cognitive domains, such as emotion (Panayiotou, 2004a, 2004b; Pavlenko, 2003, 2010), spatial relations (Park & Ziegler, 2014) and motion events (Daller et al., 2011; Flecken, 2011). The internalization of new concepts marks the beginning of the restructuring process (Pavlenko, 2014).

Coexistence

Having internalized novel ways of thinking, some L2 users manage to main-tain two or more separate sets of reference frames or conceptual categories in agreement with the typical features of each language (Pavlenko, 2011, 2016). One relevant example comes from emotion terms. Sachs and Coley (2006) explored how emotion (i.e., envy and jealousy) was represented in the bilin-guals of Russian and English. In Russian, there is a one-to-one mapping between emotion terms and actual emotions: envy (*zaviduet*) and jealousy (*revnuet*), while in English, the term *jealous* can be applied to both envy and jealousy situations. It was reported that bilinguals switched between different concepts as a function of the test language, that is, they demonstrated an English way of blurring the distinction between *jealous* and *envy* when tested in an all-in-English context while showing a Russian-like pattern in merging these two concepts when tested in an all-in-Russian context.

Similar findings have been documented in other areas of interest such as time (Bylund & Athanasopoulos, 2017), shape (Barner et al., 2009), gram-matical aspect (Athanasopoulos, Bylund et al., 2015; Bylund, 2011) and motion events (Kersten et al., 2010; Lai et al., 2014; Montero-Melis et al., 2016). For instance, Bylund and Athanasopoulos (2017) examined the impact of language learning on temporal cognition in bilingual speakers of Spanish and Swedish. When talking about time duration, Swedish prefers distance-based metaphors and describes time as 'long' and 'short', but in Spanish, duration is expressed via amount-based metaphors such as 'big' or 'small' (Casasanto, 2008, 2016; Lakoff & Johnson, 1980). Using a temporal judge-ment task, the authors concluded that Spanish–Swedish bilinguals behave differently depending on the language of operation. That is, Spanish-based prompts induced amount-based interference, but when the verbal prompts changed to Swedish, the bilinguals switched to distance-congruent interference instead. Likewise, Athanasopoulos, Bylund et al. (2015) reported similar findings in the domain of motion event construal. The study revealed that late bilinguals of German [−grammatical aspect] and English [+grammatical aspect] switched their preferences between L1- and L2-biased thinking patterns (i.e., event trajectories vs event end points) as a function of the test language. Furthermore, the language of verbal interference played a role in modulating participants' categorical preferences towards the undisrupted language, that is, bilinguals resembled German patterns when the interference occurred in English, and vice versa when it was in German. Taken together, the above-mentioned findings suggest that conceptual representations in the bilingual mind are malleable and context bound, such that speakers can switch between different thinking patterns depending on which language they are using (Wang & Li, 2019).

Convergence

The interaction between L1- and L2-based concepts is sometimes bidirectional, which has been found in both the speech and gesture production of motion in bilinguals of Spanish–Swedish (Bylund, 2011), German–French (Berthele & Stocker, 2017; Stocker & Berthele, 2020), Japanese–English (Brown & Gullberg, 2008, 2011, 2013), Chinese–English (Brown, 2015), Korean–English (Park, 2020), English–French (Engemann et al., 2012), Dutch–German (Flecken, 2011), Dutch–French (Gullberg, 2011), Turkish–German (Daller et al., 2011; Treffers-Daller & Calude, 2015) and Hungarian–English (Vanek & Hendriks, 2015). For example, Hohenstein et al. (2006) reported that when describing spontaneous motion events, the lexical choice of manner verbs in Spanish–English bilinguals fell in-between two monolingual baselines, indicating a convergence of L1- and L2-based concepts. That is, bilinguals used fewer manner verbs in their L2 compared to English monolinguals, but more manner verbs in their L1 compared to Spanish monolinguals. Similar findings came from Brown and Gullberg (2011), focusing on how Japanese learners of English conceptualized the path of motion in both languages. Using a storytelling task, this study showed that bilingual speakers displayed a unique pattern of path distribution in both their L2 and L1. In their L2, English learners used a variety of path expressions including both verb and adverbial types and demonstrated an in-between performance. In their L1, the same group of learners used more path verbs than English monolinguals, and more path adverbials than their Japanese counterparts, indicating a simultaneous bidirectional influence from L1 to L2 and L2 to L1.

Moving beyond speech, the 'in-between' performance among L2 users also comes from co-speech gestures (Brown, 2015; Brown & Gullberg, 2008; Gullberg, 2009; So, 2010). A pioneering study in this area was carried out by Brown and Gullberg (2008), who studied how Japanese intermediate learners of English speak and gesture about manner of motion in both languages. When speakers of Japanese (verb-framed) talk about the manner in speech, they are also more prone to involve manner in gestures. However, when speakers of English (satellite-framed) describe manner in speech, they gesture instead about path, a phenomenon known as manner modulation (McNeil, 2001, 2005). Results showed that Japanese learners of L2 English displayed similar verbal and gestural expressions of manner in both their L1 and L2, yet differed from monolinguals of each language. In terms of linguistic expressions, English learners expressed the information of manner significantly more often than Japanese speakers, but less frequently than their English counterparts. In terms of gestural expressions, the same group gestured about manner significantly more often than English native speakers, but less often than their Japanese counterparts. Interestingly, such bidirectional influence can even occur at moderate levels of L2 proficiency. Similar results were described by Gullberg (2009), who studied the gestural expression of placement verbs in German and Dutch learners of L2 French. The results showed that both L2 groups displayed a converging mode of conceptualization, incorporating both L1- and L2-based gesture patterns within the same utterance. Given this finding, the authors concluded that a bilingual speaker is more than the simple sum of two monolinguals in the same body, but rather an independent language user with unique linguistic and cognitive characteristics (Grosjean, 1992, 1998). This resonates with the notion of 'multicompetence' which views bilingual speakers as complete language users and direct practitioners of linguistic relativity effects (Cook, 2002, 2003, 2015).

Aside from the motion domain, another set of studies look at bidirectional cross-linguistic influence in word-to-referent mapping (Alvarado & Jameson, 2002; Ameel et al., 2009; Ameel et al., 2005; Jameson & Alvarado, 2003; Malt et al., 2016). In the case of object naming, Ameel et al. (2005) investigated naming differences between early bilinguals and monolinguals of Dutch and French for household objects (e.g., containers or dishes) in their two languages. Using an object naming and a similarity judgement task, this study showed that the naming patterns of Dutch–French bilinguals converged to a common pattern as a result of the mutual influence between these two languages. For example, the object named *fles* in Dutch has two corresponding naming patterns in French: *bouteille* and *flacon*. While the category *bouteille* refers to ordinary bottles and serves as the translation equivalent for the Dutch word *fles*, the category *flacon* exclusively refers to small bottles for perfume or tablets. The results suggested that while the use of *bouteille* and *flacon* was spread equally among French monolinguals, the bilinguals showed a preference for *bouteille* over the *fles* category, thus indicating a possible integration of these two conceptual categories in bilinguals' lexicons. A follow-up study by Ameel et al. (2009) provided further evidence about changes in the boundaries of lexical categories in bilinguals' naming patterns. That is, in order to reduce the cognitive demands of maintaining two separate conceptual categories, bilinguals seemed to 'drop' the differentiation between the exemplars (i.e., *bouteille* and *flacon*) and developed one converged set of concepts incorporating features of both languages. These findings resonate with Malt et al. (2016), who argue for 'the highly dynamic and interactive nature of bilingual representations and processing' (p. 696).

Recently, new empirical evidence from bilingual language processing provides further evidence that bilinguals tend to merge their linguistic systems and adopt a shared pattern of thinking to 'maximize common ground' in recall memory (Filipović, 2019, 2020, 2021; for a review, see Filipović & Hawkins, 2019). By exploring the cognitive domain of causation, Filipović (2020) reported that highly proficient bilinguals of Spanish and English displayed a converged mode of thinking in witness memory irrespective of the language of operation. A follow-up study by Filipović (2021) using an event encoding and a recognition memory task provided further evidence about bilingual speakers' reliance on a Spanish-based verbal encoding pattern applicable in both languages as an aid to facilitate memory recall. The author concluded that 'it is Maximising Common Ground that is in operation when both languages are active and when they share a lexicalization pattern (p. 12)'.

>To this end, it is important to bear in mind that the constant and dynamic interaction between L1 and L2 may not always lead to a converged mode of thinking. In fact, L2 users may create novel ways of carving up the world, unpredictable from the combination of both languages (Cook & Bassetti, 2011). Park and Ziegler (2014) examined the representation of spatial concepts in Korean–English bilinguals. When talking about spatial relationships between objects, English speakers make fundamental distinctions between *put in* and *put on* depending on whether the placement of an object involves containment or support. Korean speakers, in contrast, cut across the English contrasts by applying a tight-fitting and loose-fitting criterion (Bowerman & Choi, 2001, 2003). Using a non-verbal categorization task, this study showed

that bilinguals' conceptualization of space (containment vs tight-loose fit) displayed distinct and unique patterns, resembling neither L1- nor L2-based spatial concepts.

Another line of research couples language production with eye-tracking measurements to capture the dynamism between linguistic processing and attention allocation in L2 users. In a study of early Dutch–German bilinguals, Flecken (2011) applied the eye-tracking paradigms to explore how grammatical aspect affects the conceptualization of motion event construal. As stated earlier, speakers of Dutch [+grammatical aspect] do not typically mention end points when describing an ongoing event (e.g., Two women are walking), while speakers of German [−grammatical aspect] tend to mention end points more often in expressions of the same event (e.g., Two women walk towards a church). Consequently, speakers of aspect languages are less likely to direct their visual attention towards end points in comparison to those of non-aspect languages. Participants were instructed to describe a set of dynamic video clips with their eye movements being recorded. The study showed that when speaking Dutch, bilinguals tended to combine the use of progressive aspect with end points, thus demonstrating an in-between performance between the source and target languages. However, their visual attention displayed a unique pattern, diverging from Dutch monolinguals, yet not showing any signs of cross-linguistic effect from German-based patterns.

Summing up, the results suggest that when discovering the characteristics of bilinguals' linguistic and cognitive behaviour during language learning, it is very important to take into account their performances in both languages, as this can provide unique insights into the interactions between languages and how they affect cognition from a multicompetent perspective.

Restructuring towards the L2-based category

To reduce the cognitive load of maintaining different sets of concepts, L2 users may opt for an L2-based pattern in thinking and speaking. Evidence for this L2-based restructuring has been observed across different modalities in various conceptual domains, such as colour (Athanasopoulos, 2009; Athanasopoulos, Damjanovic et al., 2010), objects and substances (Cook et al., 2006; Malt & Sloman, 2003), object naming (Pavlenko & Malt, 2011), time (Lai & Boroditsky, 2013), grammatical gender (Athanosopoulos & Boutonnet, 2016; Bassetti, 2014; Kousta et al., 2008; Kurinski & Sera, 2011; Nicoladis et al., 2016), negation processing (Zhang & Vanek, 2021) and motion events (Athanasopoulos & Bylund, 2013a; Brown, 2015; Bylund et al., 2013; Stam, 2015; von Stutterheim et al., 2012).

Research on the influence of L2 on L1-based categories has been found in bilinguals' reference to end points in motion event construal. Studies by Bylund (2009a) and Bylund and Jarvis (2011), for instance, have revealed the impact of learning a non-aspect language on how end points are encoded and conceptualized in bilinguals of Spanish [+grammatical aspect] and Swedish [−grammatical aspect]. Using an oral description task, the study found that bilinguals encoded end points at a significantly higher rate in L1 Spanish compared with native Spanish speakers, thus constituting clear evidence for an L2 effect on bilinguals' event conceptualization. Bylund (2009a) further pointed out that the L2 effect on bilinguals' L1 end point encoding is modulated by their age of L2 acquisition. The argument here is that L2 influence on L1 conceptualization is more pronounced if L2 acquisition starts at an earlier stage (i.e., below the age of twelve).

In a similar vein, studies of bilingual motion descriptions also provide evidence of an L2 effect on the L1. For instance, Aveledo and Athanasopoulos (2016) examined the effect of L2 learning on the use of manner and path verbs in early Spanish–English bilinguals. The study found that the bilinguals encoded more manner verbs yet fewer path verbs in their L1 Spanish than Spanish native speakers, showing a reverse effect from the L2 on the L1. Similarly, Wang and Li (2019) found that early Cantonese–English bilinguals encoded manner significantly more often in their L1 descriptions compared to the Cantonese counterparts, thus indicating a reverse transfer from the L2 on bilinguals' conceptualization of manner and path of motion. These findings align with previous studies on the important role that L2 plays in cognitive restructuring (Brown & Gullberg, 2008; Hohenstein et al., 2006; Stocker & Berthele, 2020) and constitute clear evidence for the malleability of bilingual cognition (Athanasopoulos, Bylund et al., 2015; Bylund & Athanasopoulos, 2017; Cook, 2015).

Apart from language, L2 influence has also been observed in bilinguals' speech-accompanying gestures (Brown, 2015; Stam, 2015). Using a longitudinal design, Stam (2015) reported that a Spanish-speaking English learner's thinking and gesturing patterns about path in both languages changed over time. And the changes were most prominent after fourteen years of formal L2 instruction. Furthermore, Brown (2015) looked at linguistic and gestural expressions of manner in Chinese and Japanese learners of English. The author found that L1-based patterns for manner expressions can be restructured under the influence of the L2, even for speakers at moderate levels of proficiency. These findings suggest that looking at co-speech gestures plays an essential role in understanding the restructuring process that might not be easily manifested by looking at the verbal data alone.

As non-verbal behaviour goes, L2 influence has been found in studies of colour categorization (Athanasopoulos, 2009; Athanasopoulos et al., 2011). As mentioned earlier, cross-linguistic differences in colour vocabularies can cause differences in category boundaries or foci of colour (Franklin et al., 2008; Gilbert et al., 2006; Winawer et al., 2007). For instance, Greek has two distinct items for light and dark blue (*ghalazio* and *ble*), whereas English has only one corresponding item. Using a similarity judgement task, Athanasopoulos (2009) found that Greek–English bilinguals categorized these two shades of blue as less distinct than Greek monolinguals, thus indicating a backward effect from the L2. Furthermore, Athanasopoulos et al. (2011) extended this finding by exploring Japanese–English bilinguals' sensitivity to the distinction between blue and light blue. Like Greek, Japanese has two lexical items for blue and light blue (*mizuiro*). It was found that there was a weakening light blue/blue distinction among Japanese–English bilinguals and their overall performance was modulated by the frequency of L2 use, that is, the more frequently English was used, the less well bilinguals categorized dark blue and light blue as distinct colours.

Additionally, learning a second language with grammatical gender can boost language-induced biases in speakers whose native language lacks a gender system. In a longitudinal study, Kurinski and Sera (2011) observed that learning Spanish grammatical gender changed the way English-speaking adults categorized inanimate objects. As mentioned earlier, Spanish is a gender language whereby all nouns are assigned either a masculine or feminine gender. In contrast, English is a gender-neutral language whereby all nouns are attributed to actual biological gender. It was found that adult English learners of Spanish began to display L2-biased patterns in categorical judgements of inanimate objects after ten weeks of foreign language instruction, indicating that learning a foreign language in adulthood can bring about changes in human cognition. More recently, Athanosopoulos and Boutonnet (2016) extended Kurinski and Sera's findings (2011) by looking at how grammatical gender affects categorical judgements by adult English learners of L2 French in the context of foreign language acquisition. By employing a voice attribution technique combined with a naming task, the researchers found similar patterns of the L2 influence on L1 variety of gender attribution. In a similar vein, Kurinski et al. (2016) further reported that grammatical gender influences categorical judgements in late Hungarian–Spanish bilinguals. Results showed that bilinguals began to exhibit L2-biased categorization patterns after just a few weeks of Spanish classroom instruction. These findings, therefore, lend support to assumptions that learning a new language that has grammatical gender affects how people categorize objects, even though the learning takes place in adulthood and in the context of foreign language education.

Finally, Athanasopoulos and Bylund (2013) and Bylund et al. (2013) took cross-linguistic differences in the grammatical aspect as a point of departure and extended the effect of grammatical aspect on event categorization to the multilingual context, where a number of typologically distinct languages are frequently used in daily communication and interaction. Using a triads-matching paradigm, both studies found that native speakers of non-aspect languages such as isiXhosa and Afrikaans were less likely to base their similarity judgements on the reaching of end points in event categorization after learning an aspect language such as English. And the degree of this conceptual change was modulated by the frequency of target language use. The findings suggest that the involvement of more than two languages in language-and-thought research, although in its infancy, has the potential to provide new insights into the processes and outcomes of learning multiple languages on individual speaker's cognitive behaviour.

In sum, the overall findings provide compelling evidence that language learning influences cognitive behaviour, in different conceptual domains and across different modalities. Thus, instead of testing whether language affects bilingual cognition, the fundamental questions for researchers are (1) what factors tend to modulate this process and (2) how to uncover and explain the likely mechanisms behind this phenomenon (see Bassetti & Filipović, 2021, for an insightful discussion).

3.2 Factors Modulating the Effect of Language on Bilingual Cognition

Based on the findings reviewed earlier in the text, the degree to which language affects bilingual cognition appears to be modulated by a variety of contextual factors, such as the conceptual domain and linguistic category under investigation (i.e., structural differences vs grammatical differences), the specific type of measurement used in the task (i.e., eye-tracking, ERPs, categorization), and the extent to which the task manipulation promotes or inhibits one's access to language during cognitive processing (i.e., verbal prompt vs verbal interference; single vs dual-language context). On the other hand, a number of learner factors are also at play in modulating cognitive restructuring, including the age of onset (AO) of acquisition, based on which we can divide bilinguals into early versus late; the context of language learning, which includes naturalistic versus instructed language learning; language proficiency, which is closely related to language dominance (i.e., balanced vs unbalanced). In this section, we conduct an in-depth discussion of how these factors interact with each other in underpinning the degree of conceptual change in the bilingual mind.

3.2.1 Language Proficiency

Research on bilingual cognition suggests that among a wide variety of factors that appear to modulate the effects of language learning on bilingual development, one of the strongest predictors is the relative level of general language proficiency in each language.

On the one hand, empirical evidence shows that proficiency levels are consistently predictive of the degree of cognitive restructuring in bilingual cognition. A substantial amount of research has demonstrated that higher levels of L2 proficiency may induce greater changes in the bilingual mind in a number of conceptual domains, such as grammatical number (Athanasopoulos, 2006, 2007, 2011), grammatical gender (Kurinski & Sera, 2011; Sato et al., 2013), object naming (Ameel et al., 2005; Malt & Sloman, 2003), witness memory (Filipović, 2019, 2021; Filipović & Hawkins, 2019) and talk and gestures of motion events (Athanasopoulos, Damjanovic et al., 2015; Brown, 2015; Brown & Gullberg, 2008, 2010, 2013; Carroll et al., 2012; Park & Ziegler, 2014). For instance, Sato et al. (2013) reported that speakers of gendered languages (i.e., French) learning a gender-neutral language (i.e., English) switched between L1 and L2 gender patterns in accordance with their recent linguistic experience, and their approximation to L2-biased gender assignments was modulated by different levels of L2 proficiency. Similarly, in the domain of colour, Athanasopoulos et al. (2011) explored how colour labels affect the categorization of colour with Japanese learners of English. As mentioned earlier, Japanese has two basic lexical items for blue (light blue/blue), whereas English has only one item (blue). It was found that Japanese–English bilinguals shifted away from L1-biased patterns in the direction of the L2 as a function of increasing L2 proficiency. These findings suggest that L2 proficiency plays an important role in modulating learners' approximation to native speaker performance.

On the other hand, many studies fail to report such an effect of proficiency on bilingual development (Athanasopoulos, 2009; Bylund & Athanasopoulos, 2014a, 2015; Bylund et al., 2013; Cook et al., 2006; Daller et al., 2011; Liu, 2018; Wang, 2020; Wang & Li, 2019; Wang & Li, 2022). In recent studies, Bylund et al. (2013) and Bylund and Athanasopoulos (2014a) investigated the impact of learning an aspect language on event cognition among speakers of multiple languages (i.e., Afrikaans, isiXhosa and English). Using self-reported scores, results suggested that no proficiency effects were detected in multilinguals' categorical preferences. Instead, the day-to-day exposure to the target language exerted a significant impact on bilinguals' non-verbal behaviour. The authors argue that the lack of a proficiency effect might be ascribed to the way how language proficiency is measured (i.e., by standardized proficiency tests or self-reported scores) and in what way it is measured (i.e., general or domain-specific language proficiency).

In later studies conducted by Bylund and Athanasopoulos (2015) and Wang and Li (2021a) with highly proficient foreign language learners, and multilingual speakers also failed to document the impact of proficiency on motion event cognition. The authors attributed the findings to the assumption that the effects of proficiency on cognition are not linear, and there might be a threshold for proficiency to have a maximum effect. This argument is well supported by a body of existing evidence indicating that even moderate levels of L2 proficiency can initiate the restructuring of already-established categories in bilingual cognition (Brown, 2015; Brown & Gullberg, 2008, 2010, 2011; Cadierno, 2010; Hendriks & Hickmann, 2015;). However, once a speaker's L2 proficiency level exceeds a certain point, its effect on thought may level out subsequently (Bylund & Athanasopoulos, 2015; Cook et al., 2006).

Additionally, it is worth noticing that the impact of L2 proficiency on bilingual learning outcomes varies in accordance with other mediating variables, including age of L2 acquisition (Athanasopoulos & Kasai, 2008; Bylund, 2009b; Lai et al., 2014), language dominance (Daller et al., 2011; Filipović & Hawkins, 2019; see Treffers-Daller, 2016 for an overview), length of residence in the L2-speaking context (Athanasopoulos, 2007; Athanasopoulos et al., 2010; Park, 2020; Thierry et al., 2009) and specific domains under investigation (Brown, 2015; Brown & Gullberg, 2008, 2010, 2011; Cadierno, 2017; Tomczak & Ewert, 2015). For example, Athanasopoulos (2007) examined Japanese–English bilinguals' categorical preferences in object classification (i.e., shape or material based). Here, it was reported that both L2 proficiency and length of stay in the L2 context predicted a change towards L2-biased patterns. However, the effect of length of stay disappeared when L2 proficiency was controlled for through a partial correlation. The results suggested that length of stay affected cognitive restructuring via L2 proficiency and served as a mediating variable in predicting the degree of cognitive shift in bilingual cognition.

In summary, the aforementioned evidence indicates that the proficiency effect is a complex issue rather than a simple 'yes-no' dichotomy. In future studies, it would be worthwhile investigating in more detail the mechanisms underlying the interaction between language proficiency and other learning factors in modulating bilingual cognitive behaviour.

3.2.2 Age of L2 Acquisition

Questions regarding the AO in bilingual language-and-thought research centre on whether an early L2 onset brings better learning outcomes. Popular understanding of bilingualism indicates that early L2 acquisition could facilitate development of proper thinking patterns in the target language, given that the successful restructuring of L1 patterns might be susceptible to maturational constraints (Birdsong, 2014). However, current research suggests that it is language proficiency, rather than age of acquisition, that plays a decisive role in predicting bilinguals' ultimate achievement (Abutalebi et al., 2009; Bylund & Athanasopoulos, 2015).

Age effects on bilingual development have been documented in a variety of conceptual domains, such as time (Boroditsky, 2001; Boroditsky et al., 2003), object naming (Ameel et al., 2005; Malt & Sloman, 2003; Pavlenko & Malt, 2011), grammatical gender (Bassetti, 2007, 2011; Nicoladis et al., 2016) and motion events (Bylund, 2009a; Bylund & Jarvis, 2011; Hohenstein, 2006; Kersten et al., 2010; Lai et al., 2014; Vanek & Hendriks, 2015). For example, Boroditsky (2001) examined the conceptualization of spatial metaphors for time in Chinese–English bilinguals. The study found that bilinguals with early L2 onset showed L2 bias when thinking about time, while those who started L2 acquisition late showed bias for L1-based patterns. Likewise, using a voice attribution task, Bassetti (2007) found that Italian grammatical gender had no impact on Italian–German bilingual children, while Italian–German bilingual adults partially relied on their L1-based gender assignments when rating inanimate objects in a semantic differential task (Bassetti, 2011).

In a study with Spanish–Swedish bilinguals living in Sweden, Bylund (2009a) reported that younger L2 learners (AO<12) were more likely to transfer L2-based end point encoding patterns to the L1 compared with older learners (AO>12). The author concluded that bilingual cognition was subject to age effects in the same way as other formal language skills. In a later study, Bylund and Jarvis (2011) found that age of L2 acquisition was correlated with bilin-guals' L1 end point encoding preferences. It is concluded that earlier L2 exposure facilitates a restructuring of categorization patterns due to the neuroplasticity of the bilingual brain. These studies indicate that age effects would modulate the degree of cognitive restructuring especially for early L2 acquirers, as their L1-based grammar is not yet fully developed. As a consequence, it is more sensitive and susceptible to changes brought by the L2 (Bylund, 2011; Montrul, 2005; Pavlenko and Malt, 2011).

Despite the compelling evidence for age effects on bilingual cognition, it is worth noticing that age of L2 acquisition onset does not show as much of an effect across different contexts and learner types. It is suggested that age effects might correlate with many other factors, such as bilingual language mode, proficiency and different contexts of L2 learning (Athanasopoulos & Bylund, 2014b; Bylund, 2019). For instance, in terms of bilingual language mode, Kersten et al. (2010)

explored how Spanish–English bilinguals classified novel, moving objects and events based on the contrast of manner and path. It was found that late bilinguals (AO more than six years) switched between different ways of thinking depending on the language in use. However, early bilinguals (AO less than six years) displayed similar performance in both contexts. In a similar vein, Lai et al. (2014) examined how recent linguistic priming affected English–Spanish bilinguals' categorization preferences for voluntary motion. The authors found that late bilinguals with Spanish prompts were more prone to classify the events based on the path of motion than those with English prompts, while early bilinguals showed a converged thinking pattern independent of the test language. These findings suggest that when L2 acquisition starts in early childhood, younger speakers are more prone to develop a converged mode of thinking, incorporating language-specific cognitive behaviour of both first and second language (Ameel et al., 2005; Hohenstein, 2006; Pavlenko, 2005).

Another possible way that age of L2 onset may modulate bilingual cognition is through its joint effect with language proficiency. Athanasopoulos and Kasai (2008) examined English–Japanese bilinguals' cognitive behaviour in object categorization. Using a triads-matching task, this study found that advanced L2 speakers patterned with Japanese monolinguals in basing their judgements on shape. In contrast, intermediate L2 speakers maintained an L1-based pattern in basing their judgements on colour. At the same time, age of L2 acquisition onset was negatively correlated with one's ultimate L2 achievements. The result suggested that an early L2 onset entails a higher chance of achieving advanced proficiency, thus the age factor sometimes functions as a mediating variable in modulating the process of cognitive restructuring.

In light of the age effects in different L2 learning contexts (i.e., naturalistic or instructional settings), studies report that successful mastery of L2-specific thought patterns seems to be less conditioned by different ages of onset for instructed second language or foreign language learners, as compared with naturalistic learners (Athanasopoulos et al., 2011; Bassetti,2014; Bylund and Athanasopoulos, 2014a; Kurinski & Sera, 2011; Kurinski et al., 2016). For instance, the participants in Kersten et al. (2010) and Lai et al. (2014) were naturalistic learners with advanced proficiency levels in both languages. On the other hand, in studies that failed to report an age effect, the participants were usually instructed second language or foreign language learners (Athanasopoulos et al., 2011; Athanasopoulos, Damjanovic et al., 2015; Kurinski et al., 2016). The results are in line with Muñoz (2006, 2008), who points out that the effect of AO in naturalistic settings is partially different from that in foreign language learning settings. The differences can be attributed to a variety of methodological and contextual factors, including the amount of language exposure, intensity of exposure and types of instructions that learners receive (explicit vs implicit). In this vein, Bylund and Athanasopoulos (2014b) therefore note that, 'This illustrates the utmost importance of taking learning context into consideration when accounting for age of acquisition effects in the context of linguistic relativity' (pp. 975).

To this end, it is important to bear in mind that the age effect may play a different role in different conceptual domains under investigation. Therefore, not all studies report a significant correlation between age and bilingual cognition (Athanasopoulos, 2009; Athanasopoulos et al. 2015; Bylund & Athanasopoulos, 2015; Bassetti, 2021; Bylund et al., 2013; Liu, 2018; Malt et al., 2015; Park & Ziegler, 2014). For example, Liu (2018) examined the age effects on the comprehension of counterfactual statements in early and late Chinese–English bilinguals. While controlling for participants' proficiency levels in both languages, the study found no effects of age on L2 learners' higher- and lower-level processing of counterfactuality in the L1. Both the early and late bilinguals were able to flexibly draw on their respective L1 and L2 representational knowledge during decision-making. The overall results suggest that the age effects are selective in nature. Thus, future studies in the context of linguistic relativity are encouraged to adopt a more comprehensive perspective when addressing the dynamism between the age effect and bilingual cognition.

3.2.3 Language Context

Language context, or bilingual language mode, refers to the degree of activation of bilinguals' language or language processing mechanisms in comprehension or production (Grosjean, 1992, 1998, 2001). According to Grosjean (1998), the degree of activation of each bilinguals' languages varied from maximal to minimal, based on a number of interrelated factors such as the communicative settings, the context of language use (i.e., how many languages participants are speaking or listening during the experiment) and different degrees of language activation (i.e., single, dual language or code-switching) (Filipović & Hawkins, 2019). For this reason, language mode is usually reflected in various experiment manipulations or conditions, such as linguistic priming (Lai et al., 2014; Montero-Melis et al., 2016), language of instruction (Athanasopoulos 2007; Athanasopoulos, Bylund et al., 2015 Bylund & Athanasopoulos, 2017; Boroditsky et al., 2003; Brown & Gullberg, 2008; Kersten et al., 2010; Kousta, Vinson, & Vigliocco, 2008) and language of verbal interference (Bylund & Athanasopoulos, 2015, 2017).

On the one hand, language context has emerged as a reliable predictor for bilingual performance and its effect has been well documented in a variety of conceptual domains, such as time (Bylund & Athanasopoulos, 2017), grammatical gender (Boroditsky et al., 2003), action events (Boroditsky &Ramscar, 2002) and the domain of motion (Athanasopoulos & Albright, 2016; Athanasopoulos, Bylund et al., 2015; Kersten et al., 2010; Lai et al., 2014; Montero-Melis et al., 2016; Vanek, 2020. One such study is Boroditsky et al. (2002), who looked at how Indonesian–English bilinguals categorized action events as a function of language context. Using a memory and similarity judgement task, this study showed that bilinguals switched between L1- and L2-biased categorization patterns in accordance with the test language. Specifically, participants receiving English-biased instruction behaved more like English monolinguals compared to those having Indonesian-based instruction. Likewise, Athanasopoulos, Bylund et al. (2015), and Bylund and Athanasopoulos (2017) demonstrated a robust relationship between language context and categorization patterns. That is, the bilinguals tested in a Language A-biased context were more likely to display patterns pertaining to that language. However, when verbal interference was introduced in Language A, the bilinguals' performance switched to Language B-congruent patterns instead. Both of these studies suggested that bilinguals were capable of flexibly adapting to environment constraints and switching between language-specific thinking patterns in accordance with their recent linguistic experience, thus indicating the permeability of human cognition.

However, other studies failed to report similar effects of short-term language mediation on bilingual cognition (Athanasopoulos, 2007; Filipović, 2011, 2020; Filipović & Hawkins, 2019; Koster & Cadierno, 2019; Wang & Li, 2019). As a case in point, Athanasopoulos (2007) reported that language-biased instructions exerted no significant impact on Japanese–English bilinguals' preferences in object categorization. Similarly, Filipović (2011) showed that English–Spanish bilinguals demonstrated a converged mode of thinking and speaking of voluntary motion regardless of the test language. In a more recent study, Filipović (2020) looked at bilingual memory for causation events and found that fluent English–Spanish bilinguals with balanced proficiency levels in both languages displayed a shared pattern for the lexicalization of causation irrespective of the language in use. The results resonate well with the complex adaptive system principles model (Filipović & Hawkins, 2013, 2019), which postulates that in order to reduce the cognitive load during language processing, bilinguals tend to 'maximise common ground' between different linguistic systems to form a common linguistic pattern applicable in both languages. Therefore, as pointed out by Wang & Li (2019), whether language context has a significant impact on bilingual cognition depends on whether or not learners have established distinct sets of conceptual representations during language learning. In summary, the mixed findings suggest that bilingual mental representations are highly dynamic and context-dependent, thus providing further insights into the function of linguistic cues and the impact of language use more generally, on bilingual cognition.

3.2.4 Length of Immersion in an L2-Speaking Community

Length of immersion, or length of L2 exposure, is commonly understood as the length of residence in target-language settings (Pavlenko, 2014). In studies on the effect of the length of immersion on bilingual cognition, it has been reported that this factor has emerged as an important predictor for conceptual changes in the bilingual mind. A substantial amount of evidence suggests that on the one hand, the length of immersion is closely related to the degree of approximation to L2-based patterns (Athanasopoulos, 2009; Bylund & Athanasopoulos, 2014b; Cook et al., 2006; Tokowicz, Michael, & Kroll, 2004). In a pioneering study, Athanasopoulos et al. (2010) employed neurophysiological technology (ERP) to tap into lower-level processing and reported robust differences between Greek–English bilinguals' pre-attentive patterns in colour perception as a function of L2 immersion. The authors found that L2 learners with a longer stay in an L2-speaking country experienced reduced colour distinctions and mirrored English monolinguals in early perceptual discrimination after an average of 3.5 years of immersion. A follow-up study by Pan and Jared (2021) used neuroimaging techniques to provide further evidence about the influence of Chinese word construction on Chinese–English bilinguals' object perception preferences. Using a visual oddball paradigm, this study showed that compared with long-stay bilinguals, short-stay bilinguals differed from English monolinguals in visual mismatch negativityelicited by deviant stimuli. The robust difference between short- and long-stay bilinguals is compatible the findings of Tokowicz, Michael, and Kroll (2004), who reported that speakers immersed in the L2-speaking environment established stronger forms of word-to-referent mappings compared to those with classroom instructions only. The overall findings suggest that living in an L2-speaking environment provides learners with cumulative experiences and a specific context where target features are grounded.

Additionally, a number of studies have also shown that there is an intricate correlation between length of L2 immersion and other contextual factors, such as language dominance, proficiency and language exposure. Daller et al. (2011), for example, elaborated on the role of the length of L2 immersion and its relationship with language dominance in predicting Turkish–German bilinguals' conceptualization patterns of motion events. Two groups of bilinguals were tested: one group consisted of bilinguals living in Germany, while the other group consisted of bilingual returnees to Turkey after living in Germany for thirteen years. The task was performed in two languages and results suggested that German-resident bilinguals displayed German-like conceptualization patterns in both German and Turkish, while the returnees exhibited Turkish blueprints for conceptualization in both languages. Likewise, Park (2020) found that both L2 immersion and L2 proficiency played important roles in modulating different degrees of cognitive restructuring in Korean–English bilinguals' representations of motion events. Furthermore, while Athanasopoulos (2007) reported a significant correlation between length of stay in an L2-speaking environment and Japanese–English bilinguals' preferences for object categorization, the effect of immersion disappeared when L2 proficiency was introduced as a covariate. These findings are compatible with previous studies on the dynamic nature of cognitive restructuring. As a longer stay in an L2-speaking community may contribute to an increase in L2 proficiency and the amount of L2 exposure, these factors may be intricately interrelated with one another in predicting the development of bilingual cognition (Bylund & Athanasopoulos, 2014b).

Contrary to the aforementioned findings, it is worth noticing that not all studies identified a significant impact of length of L2 immersion on cognitive restructuring. For instance, Boroditsky (2001) examined Chinese–English bilinguals' conceptualization of time but found no significant effects of length of L2 immersion (more than ten years) on time perception. Similarly, Bylund (2009a) and Bylund and Jarvis (2011) reported no such effects in either end point encoding or sensitivity to goal-oriented motion in Spanish–Swedish bilinguals who had resided in the L2-speaking context for more than twelve years. Given these mixed findings, Bylund and Athanasopoulos (2014b) suggested that 'the factor of length of immersion in the L2 setting has been found to exert maximum effect during certain time windows' (p. 977). While Athanasopoulos et al. (2010) argued that the effect of L2 immersion can occur at a minimum period of 1.5 years, it seems that after a certain period of time (i.e., >10 years), its effect on bilingual cognition may level out subsequently (Bylund & Athanasopoulos, 2015).

To sum up, these multifaceted findings show that the interplay between language and bilingual cognition is both complex and dynamic. Thus, it is of crucial importance for researchers to take considerable variabilities among bilingual individuals into account when exploring the effects of language learning on bilingual development.

3.2.5 Language Contact

Another important factor in language-and-thought research is language contact, which refers to the total amount of time or contact bilingual speakers or L2 users have with each of their languages (Bylund & Athanasopoulos, 2014b; Pavlenko, 2014). Studies of language contact show that speakers with higher frequency of L2 use are more likely to approximate to L2 patterns, be they in colour (Athanasopoulos et al., 2011), grammatical gender (Kaushanskaya & Smith, 2016) and speech and gestures about motion (Athanasopoulos, Damjanovic et al., 2015; Bylund & Athanasopoulos, 2014a; Bylund et al., 2013; Flecken, 2011; Stam, 2010, 2015).

Language contact has been extensively examined in studies on cognitive restructuring and is commonly operationalized as language use or language exposure in the context of instructed language learning. For example, Athanasopoulos, Damjanovic et al. (2015) found a significant impact of L2 use and exposure on event categorization in English learners of German with different levels of proficiency in the context of foreign language learning. Results showed that knowledge of two or more languages with contrasting aspect systems may reduce the effects of grammatical aspect on thinking. And this process was modulated by the amount of language use and exposure to the target language. Likewise, Athanasopoulos et al. (2011) reported a significant impact of frequency of L2 use on Japanese–English bilinguals' colour perception. It was found that the more often L2 was used in daily interaction, the more likely bilinguals would shift away from their L1 and demonstrate L2-based approximations. Furthermore, this effect remained significant even after controlling for other individual factors such as L2 proficiency, age of L2 acquisition and length of L2 immersion. In a more recent study, Kaushanskaya and Smith (2016) explored the impact of learning an additional language with grammatical gender (Spanish) on a gender-neutral language (English). The findings showed that English learners with higher levels of Spanish exposure mirrored Spanish native speakers in showing high accuracy on gender-congruent pairs, while those with lower levels of L2 exposure exhibited L1-based patterns. The authors argued that sufficient use and exposure to target forms would bring about changes in the form-meaning associations in native speakers of English, even when their L2 is less proficient compared to their native language or is acquired relatively late in life.

As noted earlier, findings from bilingual cognition research clearly show that the cumulative experience that learners have in each of their languages plays a crucial role in cognitive restructuring (Bylund & Athanasopoulos, 2014a). Thus, it is of vital importance to ask further what role language contact plays in speakers with more than two languages. One influential study within this line of research comes from Bylund and Athanasopoulos (2014a), which examined how L1-isiXhosa multilinguals whose native languages lack grammatical aspect readjusted their categorical preferences of motion events after learning another language with grammatical aspect. The authors reported a clear link between the frequency of language use and the degree of cognitive restructuring, that is, the more often multilingual speakers used the aspect language, the more likely they were to shift away from the L1-based patterns. However, age of acquisition and language proficiency exerted no impact on cognitive restructuring. In a similar vein, Wang and Li (2021a) explored the impact of additional language learning on motion event cognition in Cantonese–English-Japanese multilinguals. The authors found that multilinguals demonstrated an ongoing cognitive restructuring towards L3-based patterns in both linguistic descriptions and non-linguistic categorization. The degree of the restructuring was modulated by multilinguals' contact with each of their languages. The overall findings demonstrate that for multilingual speakers who have multiple languages and live in multilingual settings, it is very important to keep track of all the languages they know as they may often have two or more L1s and multiple L2s due to their complicated learning repertoire (Bylund & Athanasopoulos, 2015b).

Despite the converging findings for the role of language contact in cognitive restructuring, it is worth mentioning that this factor is measured in different ways. For example, Wang and Li (2021a) operationalized language contact as self-reported percentage scores on a variety of daily activities, while Bylund & Athanasopoulos (2014a) relied on a Likert scale to document overall frequency of language use. In addition, recent studies have documented different types of language contact in the L2 or foreign language learning settings, such as books, radio, television and the Internet (Gullberg & Inderfrey, 2004; Schmid, 2011). Research to date has found that among different types of exposure, audiovisual input plays a fundamental role in enhancing L2 lexical and grammatical skills (Cintrón-Valentín et al., 2019; Montero Perez et al., 2018; Vanderplank, 2010). However, little is known about how these different types of language contact affect cognitive restructuring. As a pioneering study, Bylund and Athanasopoulos (2015) took a first step in examining how different types of exposure (i.e., reading, Internet, radio and television) affected cognitive restructuring in L1-Swedish learners with English as a foreign language. It was found that Swedish learners exhibited L2-based categorization patterns through exposure to English audiovisual media. The authors therefore concluded that when given sufficient multimodal input, foreign language learners were able to restructure their cognitive dispositions towards the target language. Thus, looking at different types of language contact can shed light on the mechanism of cognitive restructuring and the multimodal nature of concepts.

To sum up, the overall picture of the effects of language on cognition suggest that bilinguals' conceptual representations are dynamic and multimodal in the sense that they can be modulated by a variety of individual and contextual factors.

4 What Are the Implications for SLA?

Based on the empirical studies and theoretical frameworks reviewed above, this section focuses on whether different ways of TFS can be taught, and how the study of bilingual cognition can contribute to language learning and teaching research. We offer a detailed discussion on three pedagogical approaches to teaching motion events: contextualized learning, multimodal input and processing instructions (PIs). Our discussion mainly centres around the learnability challenges of novel concepts and the application of various teaching techniques to facilitate language learning and teaching.

4.1 Can Different Ways of Thinking-for-Speaking be Taught in SLA?

If people of different languages speak and think in different ways, what does this mean for the teaching of a second or a foreign language? While the learning difficulties for bilinguals or L2 users have been well attested across different conceptual domains, research on how to teach language-specific ways of TFS remains very limited. In a seminal article, Cook (2011) provides an insightful discussion about the relationship between linguistic relativity and teaching, namely the goals, methods, syllabi, as well as teaching techniques and reflects upon how to apply up-to-date research-based information on language and cognition research into L2 teaching and learning practices. At a general level, two questions closely related to this topic are: (1) is it desirable to include the acquisition of conceptual knowledge into the curriculum's goal and (2) what are the best ways to integrate cross-linguistic and cross-cultural differences with traditional pedagogies and practices for language teaching.

Pedagogical strategies for teaching language-specific ways of thinking and speaking mainly centre around the domain of motion, as world languages differ contrastively in how motion is talked about. As noted earlier, the acquisition of motion verbs and grammatical aspects remains challenging for L2 learners at all proficiency levels (Athanasopoulos, Damjanovic et al., 2015; Cadierno & Ruiz 2006; Hendriks & Hickmann, 2015; Pavlenko & Volynsky, 2015), as successful acquisition not only requires mastering the target linguistic forms, but also correct mappings between the semantic elements and conceptual representations. Despite the overwhelming challenges that learners have encountered, this aspect has been generally neglected in L2 course syllabus and only few studies provide empirical evidence towards the teachability of motion events (Cadierno & Robinson, 2009). For example, Stam (2015) favours the use of explicit concept-based instructions (CBIs) on information structures in L2 learning, and Bylund and Athanasopoulos (2015) suggest that multimodal input (i.e., input that combines different modes such as words, sounds and gestures) facilitate the cognitive restructuring of motion, while Laws et al. (2021) advocate the use of the Instruction Processing (IP) (VanPatten, 2004, 2015) model to promote the acquisition of language-specific thinking patterns. These innovative pedagogical approaches can provide new insights into the teachability of motion and the difficulties involved in restructuring this domain, which helps with the development of innovative pedagogical approaches, and sheds new light on the role of multimodal pedagogical tools, as well as how to use these tools to maximize cognitive changes in the classroom.

4.2 Putting Principles into Practice

4.2.1 Multimodal Language Input

As noted earlier, Bylund and Athanasopoulos (2015) reported a positive correlation between cognitive restructuring and the amount of television watched, and highlighted the role of multimodal input in L2 learning. The rationale behind this can be attributed to the multimodal nature of concepts. The assumption that concepts are multimodally constructed collaborate previous research on the benefits of multimodal pedagogies (i.e., audiovisual media) in teaching vocabulary and grammar (Blyund & Athanasopoulos, 2015; Lantolf, 2010; Peters et al., 2016). For example, research on multimodal input shows that television with subtitles or captions enhances word learning and grammar construction (Cintrón-Valentín et al., 2019; Montero Perez et al., 2018; Peters et al., 2016; Rodgers & Webb, 2017; Vanderplank, 2010). Unlike pure written or audio exposure (i.e., reading or radio listening), television has a multimodal nature that combines visuals (i.e., dynamic scenes) with sound, and sometimes on-screen texts. Based on Paivio (2014) who holds that information is visually and verbally processed through separate but related channels, combining visuals with verbal input can generally facilitate information processing, as both channels are activated simultaneously in learners' meaning-making process. This is also well supported by Mayer's (2001) cognitive theory of multimedia learning, which holds the view that 'people learn better from words and pictures than from words alone' (Mayer, 2001, p. 63). Audiovisual media, therefore, have been viewed as a powerful resource in one's L2 development (Montero Perez et al., 2018; Peters et al., 2016; Vanderplank, 2010).

In this regard, to facilitate the successful acquisition of target linguistic and conceptual frames, teachers are encouraged to adopt a multimodal teaching approach and engage L2 learners in a rich array of multimodal activities when teaching novel concepts. These pedagogical activities allow learners to construct the meaning of novel concepts in modalities that are not directly related to language (Athanasopoulos, Damjanovic et al., 2015; Blyund & Athanasopoulos, 2015). For instance, some multimodal activities involve exercises that involve the grouping or classification of the newly acquired concepts. This can help learners pay enough attention to different aspects and dimensions of the concept when developing a novel way of thinking.

In a similar vein, Brown (2015) also calls for the application of visualization strategies to engage learners in different modes of learning. Likewise, Pavlenko and Volynsky (2015) suggest replacing static pictures with videos and dynamic scenes, because 'visuals meant to provide memorable, meaningful representation for L2 learners' (Tyler, 2012, p. 136). In this regard, language teaching may benefit from combining dynamic video clips with visuals or sound, or film clips with action scenes to complement static pictures or grammatical instruction when teaching novel concepts.

4.2.2 Contextualized Learning

CBIs are grounded in the theory of developmental education originated from Vygotsky's theory of mind (Lantolf & Poehner, 2014; Vygotsky, 2012). The basic tenet of CBI is to view language as a nonmodular capacity, associated with other cognitive properties and capacities in a coordinated manner. In line with cognitive linguistics, CBI views concepts as high-quality systematic knowledge that can be acquired through contextualized learning, focused instructions that combine both linguistic and visual resources, and goal-directed activities that allow learners to use the concept in purposefully designed language-related activities (Lantolf & Poehner, 2014).

In a recent study, Stam et al. (2021) explored whether CBI could promote a full shift from the already established thinking patterns to L2-biased ones in Spanish learners of English when talking and gesturing about manner and path of motion. Participants were provided with a two-week conceptualized training following three main steps: raising awareness, introducing the concepts of motion events via visual images and videos and practicing the use and application of manner verbs in speech and gestures. Results showed that engaging learners in activities that maximized the quantity and the intensity of visual stimuli can facilitate one's re-symbolization and re-conceptualization of motion event construal, thus indicating that learners' TFS patterns could be altered even within a short period of time. The findings suggest that effective teaching and contextualized instructions attuned to the learners' needs lead to development in learners' language skills and conceptual knowledge.

4.2.3 Processing Instruction

PI plays an important role in instructed L2 classrooms (Dekeyser & Prieto Botana, 2015; Reinders & Ellis, 2009; VanPatten & Benati, 2010). It is a particular type of pedagogical intervention that seeks to alter learners away from default or less-than-optimal processing strategies and promote optimal form-meaning connections (FMCs) (VanPatten, 2004, 2015). PI is based upon a theory of learning called Input Processing, which refers to 'the initial process by which learners connect grammatical forms with their meanings' (VanPatten, 2004, p. 5). According to this model, learners use a number of parsing strategies when processing language input (VanPatten, 2004). However, during this process, learners may rely on incorrect processing-oriented principles (i.e., L1 transfer) and need to overcome erroneous default strategies in order to establish accurate and appropriate form-meaning associations. From this perspective, PI uses a particular type of input, namely the structured input (SI) practice, to disrupt learners' default processing mechanism so that learners can access the right information during language processing. PI consists of three main components: (1) L2 learners are given explicit instruction about the target form-meaning pairs and made aware of the strategies that may negatively affect their processing; (2) Referential SI activities require 'yes' or 'no' response from the learners when processing the target structure and 3) Affective SI activities provide learners with large numbers of target structures with real-world applications.

While PI has been widely used in the acquisition of grammar rules, its implementation in the conceptual domain remains very limited. In fact, PI is applicable to the teaching of novel concepts (i.e., motion events) because if learners are to be successful in acquiring L2 target structures, they need to establish language-specific processing strategies (i.e., 'map path onto the main verb') associated with the target language. As a case in point, Colasacco (2019) extends this line of research to the domain of motion events and combines this approach with principles of cognitive grammar in teaching deictic path verbs (i.e., go, come, bring and take) to Italian and German learners of L2 Spanish.

Results showed that learners who received PIs containing a component of conceptual knowledge made better FMCs and outperformed those with output-focused instruction techniques, such as the traditional instruction and meaning-based output instruction.

More recently, Laws et al. (2021) further examine the effectiveness of the IP-informed intervention on the production of manner expressions in boundary-crossing events (i.e., a man crossing the street) in L1 French learners of L2 English. As noted earlier, French is a verb-framed language and speakers of French follow the default strategy of 'map path onto the main verb' (i.e., a man entering a shop). However, such boundary-crossing constraint does not exist in English (i.e., a man walking into a shop). In this study, Laws et al. (2021) would like to test the degree to which L2 learners are able to unlearn or shift away from their L1-biased form-meaning associations towards L2-biased connections when given sufficient PIs. Using a variety of narrative elicitation tasks, this study evaluated the effectiveness of three types of instruction in constructing learners' knowledge of boundary-crossing events: (1) input-based instruction that draws on the three stages of PI; (2) input + output instruction that put emphasis on output practice and (3) explicit instruction only condition without any structured activities. The results showed a positive effect of input-based instruction over the combined approach on learners' motion event construc-tions, that is, learners with input-based instruction were more successful in unlearning the already established form-meaning associations and form L2-based connections. The results provide compelling evidence that motion events are teachable, and input-only techniques are effective in teaching complex events. The authors indicate that when teaching complex constructions in the L2, teachers need to allow learners sufficient time to feed the input into their developing linguistic system. This resonates with Flecken et al. (2015a), which suggests that long-term experience in language use can facilitate learners' mastering of novel ways of thinking and speaking in the target language.

To sum up, the acquisition of form-meaning mapping poses persistent chal-lenges for L2 learners. Language learning goes beyond the mastering of vocabulary and grammatical structures, but also interactions between grammatical construc-tions and conceptual representations of the external world. Bearing this in mind, L2 teaching may benefit from integrating language teaching with language-specific thought patterns as means to facilitate language teaching and learning.

5 What Are the New Avenues for Research?

A new avenue of research on the exploration of language learning and bilingual cognition will be discussed in connection with the ecological validity in current methodologies. In this section, we argue for moving towards a new research agenda by linking experimental methods with naturalistic data. This could help to build the missing link between lab-based experiments and naturally occurring behaviour and develop linguistic relativity in bilingual and SLA into a full research paradigm.

5.1 Moving Away from the Traditional Data: Taking the Ecological Validity into Account

In previous sections, we presented an overview of contemporary approaches on the interplay between language and its possible impact on cognition in speakers of more than one language and examined variables deemed to impact bilingual acquisition and conceptualization of L2-biased patterns during language learning. Briefly, the findings revealed the effect of language on bilingual cognition is often flexible and context-bound, depending on a variety of relevant variables including language proficiency, length of residence, language dominance, amount of language use, and experimental settings among others.

Despite the compelling evidence that has been accumulated so far, most of our current knowledge about the impact that language has on thought is based on lab-generated evidence, while little is known about how Whorfian effects can play out 'in the wild' in various communicative settings. In a seminal article, Athanasopoulos and Bylund (2020) pointed out that it is of vital importance to take the Whorfian effects out of the lab into the real world to assess one's naturally occurring behaviour and communicative strategies. This would provide a much-needed missing link between the existing experimental research and an ecologically valid approach that considers the extent to which laboratory studies generalize to natural spoken language use. Thus, it is theoretically and methodologically important to combine cognitive psychological methods with analyses of naturalistic behaviours in everyday social interactions (Leavitt 2010; Sidnell & Enfield 2012).

On the other hand, taking language-and-thought research out of the lab into the real world can also help to answer the related questions about the stability and pervasiveness of Whorfian effects across time and contexts, and pinpointing the mechanism behind how language affects cognition. For instance, although evidence suggests that the effects that language has on thought are often transient and context-dependent, it remains unclear whether such effects have pervasive and long-term consequences on one's natural behaviour in daily communicative contexts. In this regard, future research is needed to bridge these two lines of research and take language and cognition research out of the lab into the real world and back into the lab to see whether one's behavioural patterns collaborate with the other. For instance, recent advancements in cognitive sciences and neurophysiology provide us with a substantial amount of evidence validating that the basic aspectual distinctions across languages affect speakers' view frames of event temporality in spatial cognition by using psychological and neurophysiological research paradigms, such as triads-matching, eye-tracking and ERPs (Athanasopoulos, Damjanovic et al., 2015; Flecken et al., 2015b; von Stutterheim et al., 2012, see Athanasopoulos & Casaponsa, 2020, for a review). However, it remains unclear how people in real life express and conceptualize spatial concepts, whether language-specific ways of thinking are robust across time and context, or susceptible to immediate language use and assessment conditions. To further explore the validity and significance of the experimental findings of spatial cognition, further research is very much needed in taking a multidisciplinary approach that combines linguistic ethnography and experiment methods to gain a fuller picture of the relativistic effects.

5.2 Adopting a Mixed-Methods Approach

Another important issue is about what types of methods should be used to study the intriguing interactions between language and its impact on cognition. While most of the current research relies on experimental approaches and behavioural measures to elicit quantitative data, little has been done to explore relativistic effects using qualitative methodology. However, given the complexities between language–and–thought interface, it is very important to bring together different types of methods and adopt a mixed-methods approach (Bassetti & Filipović, 2021). For instance, Bassetti (2007) explored the effect of grammatical gender on Italian–German bilinguals' object categorization. Participants completed a voice attribution task, a typical experimental method in gender research, and then moved on to answering open-ended questions concerning their sorting criteria used for voice assignment and whether they were aware of contrasts in how different languages conceptualize gender. Results showed that although participants did not differ considerably in their categorical selections, their answers to the questions provided a more nuanced picture of their thinking process.

In a more recent study, Pavlenko et al. (2017) used semi-structured interviews to elicit verbal descriptions of visual stimuli (i.e., pictures and real paintings) containing different hues and shades of blue in speakers of Russian (i.e., goluboj for light/sky blue; sinij for dark/navy blue), English (i.e., one basic term blue) and Ukrainian (i.e., blakytnyj and golubyj for light/sky blue; synij for dark/navy blue).

Compared to the standard colour charts (i.e., Munsell colour array) typically used in colour research, incorporating a qualitative design has its potential to provide more fine-grained detail on where and how language-specific patterns of colour reference affect the salience of colour categories in the speaker's mind. It is found that speakers of different languages were perceptually aware of the distinctions between different shades of blues and able to talk about them. However, compared to English speakers who habitually replied on one single lexical term to describe different types of blue (i.e., the blue window), Russian speakers systematically drew on both dark blue (sinij) and light blue (goluboj) with modifiers (i.e., svetlo-goluboj/light-light blue), thus indicating that Russian speakers displayed a more prominent communicative salience of the *sinij/goluboj* contrast. This study indicated that adopting a mixed-methods approach could shed more light on the interaction between colour naming and categorization pattern in speakers' mind, by asking them to describe their thought directly.

The overall findings suggest that adopting a mixed-methods approach could help researchers move beyond traditional categorization and perception paradigms and start looking at data from various sources, such as semi-structured interviews, introspective methods (i.e., stimulated recall), observations and text analysis. Further research may take advantage of this approach and use more ecologically valid stimuli, to obtain corroborating evidence for participants' behaviours in experimental contexts. This may broaden the scope of language-and-thought research to measurable social interactional and cultural effects.

5.3 Multilingualism

Despite compelling evidence from psychological experiments that our understanding of reality and the world is mediated by language-specific categories made available in our language(s), several issues regarding the language-and-thought debate are still waiting to be resolved. For instance, the evidence we have now obtained is largely based on the investigation of monolingual speakers through cross-linguistic and cross-cultural comparisons. However, studies involving speakers of two or more languages (i.e., multilinguals) remain very limited (Bylund & Athanasopoulos, 2014b; Lucy, 2016). Given that multilingualism has become a social norm (Aronin & Singleton, 2012), and multilingual speakers display unique linguistic and cognitive characteristics (Cook & Li, 2016), extending language-and-thought research into multilingualism is deemed as a natural extension. The dialogue between multilingualism and relativity research can help assess how multiple languages affect thought together: whether multilingual speakers have developed separate concepts for each language, or they have one single integrated way of thinking.

In a very recent study, Wang and Li (2021a) examined how Cantonese–English–Japanese multilingual lexicalized and conceptualized motion events by manipulating different language contexts. Combining both online processing measures (reaction times) and offline processing measures (language production and event categorization), this study showed that access to different languages allows multilinguals to access different mental representations, depending on which language they speak. The study furthermore suggested that the amount of language learning matters, with linguistic proficiency and language use moderating the possible effects of language on thought. The findings thus indicate that the influence that language has on thought is often transient, thus showing the dynamics between language learning and malleability of human cognition.

The dialogue between multilingualism and linguistic relativity research is both theoretically and methodologically important. On the research side, it will shed light on the complexity of cognitive effects in the multilingual mind and the diverse mechanisms underlying the effects of multiple language learning. Methodologically speaking, to be effective, researchers studying relativity effects with multilinguals need to keep track of speakers' language learning trajectories, such as the age of acquisition, language dominance and the distribution of contact across different languages, as there are often more than two L1s or L2s involved (Bylund & Athanasopoulos, 2014b).

5.4 Translanguaging and Thought

In addition to what has been reviewed earlier in this Element, a new line of inquiry about the relationship between language and thought has been pursued through a translanguaging lens (Li, 2018). Translanguaging concerns the complex and dynamic linguistic practices of bilingual and multilingual language users. Accepting the I-language and E-language distinction, translanguaging sees named languages such as English, Spanish and Chinese as historico-political constructs. What we normally call bilinguals and multilinguals are people who have been socialized into using two or more named languages in specific contexts and mix and switch between them as they wish for communicative purposes. Bilinguals and multilinguals do not, however, have two or more thoughts, each attached to a named language. Such an argument may seem to contradict a great deal of what has been discussed earlier in this Element. But the translanguaging perspective makes a fine but very important distinction between thought and ways of thinking. Ways of thinking are externalizations and individualizations of thought and are influenced by socialization. The individual ways of thinking are often articulated through named languages, much like the way Slobin suggests in the TFS model. Bilinguals and multilinguals can express different ways of thinking, through different named languages. But thought transcends named languages. Concerned primarily with the habitual mixing and switching between different named languages that bilinguals typically do in everyday social interaction, Li (2018) argues that bilinguals do not think unilingually in a named language. Furthermore, following a distributed cognition perspective, thinking is embodied and multimodal. To test the theoretical positions of the translanguaging perspective, it is important to focus on bilinguals and multilinguals in the bilingual mode, that is, when they are engáging in fluid language mixing and switching, and their ability to draw on elements of different named languages and indeed other semiotic systems to express their thoughts, rather than comparing one language and thought at a time.

5.5 Conclusion

In sum, we have proposed that future research needs to extend boundaries of language-and-thought research from monolingualism to multilingualism by viewing speakers with more than one language as multicompetent individuals with unique linguistic and cognitive features. By taking the ecological validity into account and advocating a multidisciplinary approach towards the Whorfian effects, we hope that future research will progressively unveil the intricate relationship between language(s) and aspects of cognition in the context of bilingual and SLA.

References

Abutalebi, J., Cappa, S. F., & Perani, D. (2009). What can functional neuro-imaging tell us about the bilingual brain? In J. F. Kroll & A. M. B. de Groot (Eds.), *Handbook of bilingualism* (pp. 497–515). Oxford: Oxford University Press.

Abutalebi, J., & Green, D. W. (2008). Control mechanisms in bilingual language production: neural evidence from language switching studies. *Language and Cognitive Processes, 24,* 557–582.

Allen, S., Özyürek, A., Kita, S. et al. (2007). Language-specific and universal influences in children's syntactic packaging of manner and path: A comparison of English, Japanese, and Turkish. *Cognition, 102*(1), 16–48.

Alverson, H. (1994). *Semantics and experience: Universal metaphors of time in English, Mandarin, Hindi, and Sesotho.* Baltimore: Johns Hopkins University Press.

Alvarado, N., & Jameson, K. (2002). The use of modifying terms in the naming and categorization of color appearances in Vietnamese and English. *Journal of Cognition and Culture, 2*(1), 53–80.

Ameel, E., Malt, B. C., Storms, G., & Van Assche, F. (2009). Semantic convergence in the bilingual lexicon. *Journal of Memory and Language, 60*(2), 270–290.

Ameel, E., Storms, G., Malt, B., & Sloman, S. (2005). How bilinguals solve the naming problem. *Journal of Memory and Language, 52,* 309–329.

Athanasopoulos, P. (2006). Effects of the grammatical representation of number on cognition in bilinguals. *Bilingualism: Language and Cognition, 9,* 89–96.

Athanasopoulos, P. (2007). Do bilinguals think differently from monolinguals? Evidence from non-linguistic cognitive categorisation of objects in Japanese-English bilinguals. *Selected Papers on Theoretical and Applied Linguistics, 17*(2), 338–345.

Athanasopoulos, P. (2009). Cognitive representation of colour in bilinguals: The case of Greek blues. *Bilingualism: Language and Cognition, 12*(1), 83–95.

Athanasopoulos, P. (2016). Premises of multi-competence. In V. Cook & W. Li (Eds.), *The Cambridge handbook of linguistic multi-competence* (pp. 355–375). New York: Cambridge University Press.

Athanasopoulos, P., & Albright, D. (2016). A perceptual learning approach to the Whorfian hypothesis: Supervised classification of motion. *Language Learning, 66*(3), 666–689.

Athanosopoulos, P., & Boutonnet, B. (2016). Learning grammatical gender in a second language changes categorization of inanimate objects: Replications and new evidence from English learners of L2 French. In R. Alonso (Eds.), *Crosslinguistic influence in second language acquisition* (pp.173–192). Bristol, Blue Ridge Summit: Multilingual Matters.

Athanasopoulos, P., & Bylund, E. (2013a). Does grammatical aspect affect motion event cognition? A cross-linguistic comparison of English and Swedish speakers. *Cognitive Science, 37*(2), 286–309.

Athanasopoulos, P., & Bylund, E. (2013b). The 'thinking' in thinking-for-speaking: Where is it? *Language, Interaction and Acquisition, 4*(1), 91–100.

Athanasopoulos, P., & Bylund, E. (2020). Whorf in the wild: Naturalistic evidence from human interaction. *Applied Linguistics, 41*(6), 947–970.

Athanasopoulos, P., Bylund, E., & Casasanto, D. (2016). Introduction to the special issue: New and interdisciplinary approaches to linguistic relativity. *Language Learning, 66*(3), 482–486.

Athanasopoulos, P., Bylund, E., Montero-Melis, G. et al. (2015). Two languages, two minds: Flexible cognitive processing driven by language of operation. *Psychological Science, 26*(4), 518–526.

Athanasopoulos, P., & Casaponsa, A. (2020). The Whorfian brain: Neuroscientific approaches to linguistic relativity. *Cognitive Neuropsychology, 37*(5–6), 393–412.

Athanasopoulos, P., Damjanovic, L., Burnand, J., & Bylund, E. (2015). Learning to think in a second language: Effects of proficiency and length of exposure in English learners of German. *Modern Language Journal, 99*(S1), 138–153.

Athanasopoulos, P., Damjanovic, L., Krajciova, A., & Sasaki, M. (2011). Representation of colour concepts in bilingual cognition: The case of Japanese blues. *Bilingualism: Language and Cognition, 14*(1), 9–17.

Athanasopoulos, P., Dering, B., Wiggett, A., Kuipers, J.-R., & Thierry, G. (2010). Perceptual shift in bilingualism: Brain potentials reveal plasticity in pre-attentive colour perception. *Cognition, 116*(3), 437–443.

Athanasopoulos, P., & Kasai, C. (2008). Language and thought in bilinguals: The case of grammatical number and nonverbal classification preferences. *Applied Psycholinguistics, 29*(1), 105–123.

Aronin, L., & Singleton, D. (2012). *Multilingualism.* Amsterdam: John Benjamins.

Aske, J. (1989). Path predicates in English and Spanish: A closer look. *Annual Meeting of the Berkeley Linguistics Society, 15*, 1–14.

Baddeley, A. (2003). Working memory and language: An overview. *Journal of Communication Disorders, 36*(3), 189–208.

Bassetti, B. (2007). Bilingualism and thought: Grammatical gender and concepts of objects in Italian-German bilingual children. *International Journal of Bilingualism*, *11*(3), 251–273.

Bassetti, B. (2011). The grammatical and conceptual gender of animals in second language users. In V. J. Cook & B. Bassetti (Eds.), *Language and bilingual cognition* (pp. 357–384). Oxford: Psychology Press.

Bassetti, B. (2014). Is grammatical gender considered arbitrary or semantically motivated? Evidence from monolinguals, second language learners and early bilinguals. *British Journal of Psychology*, *105*(2), 273–294.

Bassetti, B., & Cook, V. (2011). Language and cognition: The second language user. In V. J. Cook & B. Bassetti (Eds.), *Language and bilingual cognition* (pp. 143–190). Oxford: Psychology Press.

Bassetti, B., & Filipović, L. (2021). Researching language and cognition in bilinguals. *International Journal of Bilingualism*. http://doi.org/1367006921 1022860.

Bassetti, B., & Nicoladis, E. (2016). Research on grammatical gender and thought in early and emergent bilinguals. *International Journal of Bilingualism*, *20*(1), 3–16.

Barner, D., Inagaki, S., & Li, P. (2009). Language, thought, and real nouns. *Cognition*, *111*(3), 329–344.

Bender, A., Beller, S., & Klauer, K. C. (2018). Gender congruency from a neutral point of view: The roles of gender classes and conceptual connotations. *Journal of Experimental Psychology: Learning, Memory, and Cognition*, *44*(10), 1580.

Berman, R. A., & Slobin, D. I. (1994). Narrative structure. In R. A. Berman & D. I. Slobin (Eds.), *Relating events in narrative: A crosslinguistic developmental study* (Vol. 39, p. 84). Hillsdale: Lawrence Erlbaum.

Berthele, R., & Stocker, L. (2017). The effect of language mode on motion event descriptions in German–French bilinguals. *Language and Cognition, 9* (4), 648–676.

Bialystok, E. (2009). Bilingualism: The good, the bad, and the indifferent. *Bilingualism: Language and Cognition*, *12*(1), 3–11.

Boroditsky, L., & Ramscar, M. (2002). The roles of body and mind in abstract thought. *Psychological Science*, *13*(2), 185–189.

Boroditsky, L., Schmidt, L. A., & Phillips, W. (2003). Sex, syntax, and semantics. In D. Gentner & S. Goldin-Meadow (Eds.), *Language in mind: Advances in the study of language and thought* (pp. 61–79). Cambridge, MA: MIT Press.

Bowerman, M., & Choi, S. (2001). Shaping meanings for language: universal and language-specific in the acquisition of spatial semantic categories. In

M. Bowerman, S. C. Levinson & S. Levinson (Eds.). *Language acquisition and conceptual development* (pp. 475–511). Cambridge: Cambridge University Press.

Bowerman, M., & Choi, S. (2003). Space under construction: Language-specific spatial categorization in first language acquisition. In D. Gentner & S. Goldin-Meadow (Eds.), *Language in mind: Advances in the study of language and thought* (pp. 387–427). Cambridge, MA: MIT Press.

Birdsong, D. (2014). Dominance and age in bilingualism. *Applied Linguistics*, *35*(4), 374–392.

Booth, A. E., & Waxman, S. R. (2002). Word learning is 'smart': Evidence that conceptual information affects preschoolers' extension of novel words. *Cognition, 84*, B11–B22.

Boroditsky, L. (2001). Does language shape thought? Mandarin and English speakers' conceptions of time. *Cognitive Psychology, 43*(1), 1–22.

Boroditsky, L., Fuhrman, O., & McCormick, K. (2011). Do English and Mandarin speakers think about time differently? *Cognition, 118*(1), 123–129.

Boroditsky, L., Schmidt, L. A., & Phillips, W. (2003). Sex, syntax, and semantics. In S. Gentner & S. Goldin-Meadow (Eds.), *Language in mind: Advances in the study of language and thought* (pp. 61–79). Cambridge, MA: MIT Press.

Boutonnet, B., Athanasopoulos, P., & Thierry, G. (2012). Unconscious effects of grammatical gender during object categorisation. *Brain Research, 1479*, 72–79.

Boutonnet, B., Dering, B., Viñas-Guasch, N., & Thierry, G. (2013) Seeing objects through the language glass. *Journal of Cognitive Neuroscience 25*, 1702–1710.

Brown, A. (2015). Universal development and L1-L2 convergence in bilingual construal of manner in speech and gesture in Mandarin, Japanese, and English. *Modern Language Journal, 99*(S1), 66–82.

Brown, A., & Gullberg, M. (2008). Bidirectional cross-linguistic influence in L1-L2 encoding of manner in speech and gesture: A study of Japanese speakers of English. *Studies in Second Language Acquisition, 30*(2), 225–251.

Brown, A., & Gullberg, M. (2010). Changes in encoding of path of motion in a first language during acquisition of a second language. *Cognitive Linguistics, 21*(2), 263–286.

Brown, A., & Gullberg, M. (2011). Bidirectional cross-linguistic influence in event conceptualization? Expressions of path among Japanese learners of English. *Bilingualism: Language and Cognition, 14*(1), 79–94.

Brown, A., & Gullberg, M. (2013). L1-L2 convergence in clausal packaging in Japanese and English. *Bilingualism: Language and Cognition, 16*(3), 477–494.

Brown, R., & Lenneberg, E. H. (1954). A study of language and cognition. *Journal of Abnormal and Social Psychology, 49*, 454–462.

Bylund, E. (2009a). Effects of age of L2 acquisition on L1 event conceptualization patterns. *Bilingualism: Language and Cognition, 12*(3), 305–322.

Bylund, E. (2009b). Maturational constraints and first language attrition. *Language Learning, 59*(3), 687–715.

Bylund, E. (2011). Segmentation and temporal structuring of events in early Spanish-Swedish bilinguals. *International Journal of Bilingualism, 15*(1), 56–84.

Bylund, E. (2018). Interpreting age effects in language acquisition and attrition. *Linguistic Approaches to Bilingualism, 7*(6), 682–685.

Bylund, E. (2019). Age effects in language attrition. In M. S. Schmid & B. Köpke (Eds.), *The Oxford handbook on language attrition* (pp. 277–287). Oxford: Oxford University Press.

Bylund, E., & Athanasopoulos, P. (2014a). Language and thought in a multilingual context: The case of isiXhosa. *Bilingualism: Language and Cognition, 17*(2), 431–441.

Bylund, E., & Athanasopoulos, P. (2014b). Linguistic relativity in SLA: Toward a new research program. *Language Learning, 64*(4), 952–985.

Bylund, E., & Athanasopoulos, P. (2017). The Whorfian time warp: Representing duration through the language hourglass. *Journal of Experimental Psychology: General, 146*(7), 911–916.

Bylund, E., & Athanasopoulos, P. (2015). Televised Whorf: Cognitive restructuring in advanced foreign language learners as a function of audiovisual media exposure. *Modern Language Journal, 99*, 123–137.

Bylund, E., Athanasopoulos, P., & Oostendorp, M. (2013). Motion event cognition and grammatical aspect: Evidence from Afrikaans. *Linguistics: An Interdisciplinary Journal of the Language Sciences, 51*(5), 929–955.

Bylund, E., & Jarvis, S. (2011). L2 effects on L1 event conceptualization. *Bilingualism: Language and Cognition, 14*(1), 47–59.

Cadierno, T. (2008). Learning to talk about motion in a foreign language. In P. Robinson & N. C. Ellis (Eds.), *Handbook of cognitive linguistics and second language acquisition* (pp. 239–275). London: Routledge.

Cadierno, T. (2010). Motion in Danish as a second language: Does the learner's L1 make a difference? In Z. Han & T. Cadierno (Eds.), *Linguistic relativity in SLA: Thinking for speaking* (pp. 1–33). Bristol: Multilingual Matters.

Cadierno, T. (2017). Thinking for speaking about motion in a second language: Looking back and forward. In I. Ibarretxe-Antuñano (Ed.), *Motion and space across languages and applications* (pp. 279–300). Amsterdam: John Benjamins.

Cadierno, T., & Robinson, P. (2009). Language typology, task complexity and the development of L2 lexicalization patterns for describing motion events. *Annual Review of Cognitive Linguistics, 7*(1), 245–276.

Cadierno, T., & Ruiz, L. (2006). Motion events in Spanish L2 acquisition. *Annual Review of Cognitive Linguistics, 4*(1), 183–216.

Carroll, M., von Stutterheim, C., & Nüse, R. (2011). The language and thought debate: A psycholinguistic approach. In T. Pechmann & C. Habel (Eds.), *Multidisciplinary approaches to language production* (pp. 183–218). Berlin/ New York: De Gruyter Mouton.

Carroll, M., Weimar, K., Flecken, M., Lambert, M., & von Stutterheim, C. (2012). Tracing trajectories: Motion event construal by advanced L2 French-English and L2 French-German speakers. *LIA Language, Interaction and Acquisition, 3*(2), 202–230.

Casasanto, D. (2008). Who's afraid of the big bad Whorf? Crosslinguistic differences in temporal language and thought. *Language Learning, 58*, 63–79.

Casasanto, D. (2015). Linguistic relativity. In N. Riemer (Ed.), *The Routledge handbook of semantics* (pp. 174–190). London: Routledge.

Casasanto, D. (2016). A shared mechanism of linguistic, cultural, and bodily relativity. *Language Learning, 66*(3), 714–730.

Casasanto, D., & Boroditsky, L. (2008). Time in the mind: Using space to think about time. *Cognition, 106*(2), 579–593.

Casasanto, D., Boroditsky, L., Phillips, W. et al. (2004). How deep are effects of language on thought? Time estimation in speakers of English, Indonesian, Greek, and Spanish. *Proceedings of the Annual Meeting of the Cognitive Science Society, 26*(26), 186–191.

Chamorro, G., Sorace, A., & Sturt, P. (2016). What is the source of L1 attrition? The effect of recent L1 re-exposure on Spanish speakers under L1 attrition. *Bilingualism: Language and Cognition, 19*(3), 520–532.

Choi, S., & Bowerman, M. (1991). Learning to express motion events in English and Korean: The influence of language-specific lexicalization patterns. *Cognition, 41*(1–3), 83–121.

Chomsky, N. (1975). *Reflections on language*. London: Temple Smith.

Cintrón-Valentín, M., García-Amaya, L., & Ellis, N. C. (2019). Captioning and grammar learning in the L2 Spanish classroom. *The Language Learning Journal, 47*(4), 439–459.

Colasacco, M. A. (2019). A cognitive approach to teaching deictic motion verbs to German and Italian students of Spanish. *IRAL-International Review of Applied Linguistics in Language Teaching, 57*(1), 71–95.

Comrie, B. (1976) *Aspect*. New York: Cambridge University Press.

Cook, V. (1991). The poverty of the stimulus argument and multicompetence. *Second Language Research, 7*(2), 103–117.

Cook, V. (1992). Evidence for multicompetence. *Language Learning, 42*(4), 557–591.

Cook, V. (1999). Going beyond the native speaker in language teaching. *TESOL Quarterly, 33*, 185–209.

Cook, V. (2002). Background to the L2 user. In V. Cook (Ed.), *Portraits of the L2 user* (pp. 1–28). Clevedon: Multilingual Matters.

Cook, V. (2003). The changing L1 in the L2 user's mind. In V. J. Cook (Ed.), *Effects of the second language on the first* (pp. 1–18). Clevedon: Multilingual Matters.

Cook, V. (2011). Teaching English as a foreign language in Europe. In E. Hinkel (Ed.), *Handbook of research in second language teaching and learning* (pp. 140–154). New York: Routledge.

Cook, V. (2015). Discussing the language and thought of motion in second language speakers. *The Modern Language Journal, 99*(S1), 154–164.

Cook, V. (2016). Premises of multi-competence. In V. Cook & W. Li (Eds.), *The Cambridge handbook of linguistic multi-competence* (pp. 1–25). New York: Cambridge University Press.

Cook, V., Bassetti, B., Kasai, C., Sasaki, M., & Takahashi, J. A. (2006). Do bilinguals have different concepts? The case of shape and material in Japanese L2 users of English. *International Journal of Bilingualism, 10*(2), 137–152.

Cook, V., & Li, W. (2016). *Cognitive consequences of multi-competence.* Cambridge: Cambridge University Press.

Dahl, Ö. (2000). The tense-aspect systems of European languages in a typological perspective. In Ö. Dahl, (Ed.), *Tense and aspect in the languages of Europe* (pp. 3–26). Berlin, New York: Mouton de Gruyter.

Daller, M. H., Treffers-Daller, J., & Furman, R. (2011). Transfer of conceptualization patterns in bilinguals: The construal of motion events in Turkish and German. *Bilingualism: Language and Cognition, 14*(1), 95–119.

Dekeyser, R., & Prieto Botana, G. (2015). The effectiveness of processing instruction in L2 grammar acquisition: A narrative review. *Applied Linguistics, 36*(3), 290–305.

Dolscheid, S., Shayan, S., Majid, A., & Casasanto, D. (2013). The thickness of musical pitch: Psychophysical evidence for linguistic relativity. *Psychological Science, 24*(5), 613–621.

Duncan, S. (2001). Co-expressivity of speech and gesture: Manner of motion in Spanish, English, and Chinese. *Annual Meeting of the Berkeley Linguistics Society, 27*(1), 353–370.

Engemann, H., Harr, A.-K., & Hickmann, M. (2012). Caused motion events across languages and learner types: A comparison of bilingual first and adult second language acquisition. In L. Filipović & K. M. Jaszczolt (Eds.), *Space and time in languages and cultures* (pp. 263–288). Amsterdam, Netherlands: John Benjamins.

Ervin, S. M. (1961). Semantic shift in bilingualism. *The American Journal of Psychology, 74*(2), 233–241.

Ervin-Tripp, S. (2011). Advances in the study of bilingualism: A personal view. In V. Cook & B. Bassetti (Eds.), *Language and bilingual cognition* (pp. 219–228). New York: Psychology Press.

Evans, V. (2004). How we conceptualise time: Language, meaning and temporal cognition. In V. Evans, B. K. Bergen, & J. Zinken, (Eds.), *The cognitive linguistics reader* (pp. 733–765). London: Equinox Publishing.

Filipović, L. (2021). First language versus second language effect on memory for motion events: The role of language type and proficiency. *International Journal of Bilingualism*. http://doi.org/10.1177/13670069211022863.

Filipović, L. (2020). Bilingual memory advantage: Bilinguals use a common linguistic pattern as an aid to recall memory. *International Journal of Bilingualism, 24*(3), 542–555.

Filipović, L. (2018). Speaking in a second language but thinking in the first language: Language-specific effects on memory for causation events in English and Spanish. *International Journal of Bilingualism, 22*(2), 180–198.

Filipović, L. (2011). Speaking and remembering in one or two languages: Bilingual vs. monolingual lexicalization and memory for motion events. *International Journal of Bilingualism, 15*(4), 466–485.

Filipović, L., & Hawkins, J. A. (2013). Multiple factors in second language acquisition: The CASP model. *Linguistics 51* (1), 145–176.

Filipović, L., & Hawkins, J. A. (2019). The complex adaptive system principles model for bilingualism: Language interactions within and across bilingual minds. *International Journal of Bilingualism, 23*(6), 1223–1248.

Filipović, L., & Ibarretxe-Antuñano, I. (2015). Motion. In E. Dąbrowska & D. Dagmar (Eds.), *Handbook of cognitive linguistics* (pp. 527–545). Berlin/ Boston: De Gruyter Mouton .

Finkbeiner, M., Nicol, J., Greth, D., & Nakamura, K. (2002). The role of language in memory for actions. *Journal of Psycholinguistic Research, 31*(5), 447–457.

Flecken, M. (2011). Event conceptualization by early Dutch-German bilinguals: Insights from linguistic and eye-tracking data. *Bilingualism: Language and Cognition, 14*(1), 61–77.

Flecken, M., Athanasopoulos, P., Kuipers, J. R., & Thierry, G. (2015a). On the road to somewhere: Brain potentials reflect language effects on motion event perception. *Cognition, 141*, 41–51.

Flecken, M., Carroll, M., Weimar, K., & von Stutterheim, C. (2015b). Driving along the road or heading for the village? Conceptual differences underlying motion event encoding in French, German, and French-German L2 users. *Modern Language Journal, 99*(S1), 100–122.

Flecken, M., Gerwien, J., Carroll, M., & von Stutterheim, C. (2015c). Analyzing gaze allocation during language planning: A cross-linguistic study on dynamic events. *Language and Cognition, 7*(1), 138–166.

Flecken, M., von Stutterheim, C., & Carroll, M. (2014). Grammatical aspect influences motion event perception: Findings from a cross- linguistic non-verbal recognition task. *Language and Cognition, 6*(1), 45–78.

Franklin, A., Drivonikou, G. V., Bevis, L. et al. (2008). Categorical perception of color is lateralized to the right hemisphere in infants, but to the left hemisphere in adults. *Proceedings of the National Academy of Sciences of the United States of America, 105*, 3221–3225.

Fuhrman, O., McCormick, K., Chen, E. et al. (2011). How linguistic and cultural forces shape conceptions of time: English and Mandarin time in 3D. *Cognitive Science, 35*(7), 1305–1328.

Gallistel, C. R. (1989). Animal cognition: The representation of space, time and number. *Annual Review of Psychology, 40*(1), 155–189.

Gennari, S. P., Sloman, S. A., Malt, B. C., & Fitch, W. T. (2002). Motion events in language and cognition. *Cognition, 83*(1), 49–79.

Gilbert, A. L., Regier, T., Kay, P., & Ivry, R. B. (2006). Whorf hypothesis is supported in the right visual field but not the left. *Proceedings of the National Academy of Sciences, 103*(2), 489–494.

Goldstone, R. L., & Kersten, A. (2003). Concepts and categories. In A. F. Healy & R. W. Proctor (Eds.), *Comprehensive handbook of psychology: Experimental psychology* (pp. 599–621). New York: Wiley.

Grosjean, F. (1992). Another view of bilingualism. In R. J. Harris (Ed.), *Cognitive processing in bilinguals* (pp. 51–62). Amsterdam: North Holland.

Grosjean, F. (1998). Studying bilinguals: Methodological and conceptual issues. *Bilingualism: Language and Cognition, 1*(2), 131–149.

Grosjean, F. (2001). The bilingual's language modes. In Nicol, J. (Ed.), *One mind, two languages: Bilingual language processing* (pp. 1–22). Oxford: Blackwell.

Gu, Y., Mol, L., Hoetjes, M., & Swerts, M. (2017). Conceptual and lexical effects on gestures: the case of vertical spatial metaphors for time in Chinese. *Language, Cognition and Neuroscience, 32*(8), 1048–1063.

Gullberg, M. (2009). Reconstructing verb meaning in a second language: How English speakers of L2 Dutch talk and gesture about placement. *Annual Review of Cognitive Linguistics*, *7*, 222–245

Gullberg, M. (2011). Thinking, speaking, and gesturing about motion in more than one language. In A. Pavlenko (Ed.), *Thinking and speaking in two languages* (pp. 143–169). Bristol: Multilingual Matters.

Gullberg, M., & Indefrey, P. (2003). *Language Background Questionnaire. The Dynamics of Multilingual Processing*. Nijmegen: Max Planck Institute for Psycholinguistics.

Han, Z., & Cadierno, T. (2010). *Linguistic relativity in SLA: Thinking for speaking*. Bristol: Multilingual Matters.

Hendriks, H., & Hickmann, M. (2015). Finding one's path into another language: On the expression of boundary crossing by English learners of French. *Modern Language Journal*, *99*(S1), 14–31.

Hickmann, M., & Hendriks, H. (2006). Static and dynamic location in French and in English. *First Language*, *26*(1), 103–135.

Hickmann, M., & Hendriks, H. (2010). Typological constraints on the acquisition of spatial language in French and English. *Cognitive Linguistics*, *21*(2), 189–215.

Hickmann, M., Taranne, P., & Bonnet, P. (2009). Motion in first language acquisition: Manner and path in French and English child language. *Journal of Child Language*, *36*(4), 705–741.

Hohenstein, J., Eisenberg, A., & Naigles, L. (2006). Is he floating across or crossing afloat? Cross-influence of L1 and L2 in Spanish-English bilingual adults. *Bilingualism: Language and Cognition*, *9*(3), 249–261.

Imai, M., & Gentner, D. (1997). A cross-linguistic study of early word meaning: Universal ontology and linguistic influence. *Cognition*, *62*, 169–200.

Jameson, & Alvarado, N. (2003). Differences in colour naming and colour salience in Vietnamese and English. *Colour Research and Application*, *28*(2), 113–138.

Jarvis, S. (2007). Theoretical and methodological issues in the investigation of conceptual transfer. *Vigo International Journal of Applied Linguistics*, *4*, 43–71

Jarvis, S. (2011). Conceptual transfer: Crosslinguistic effects in categorization and construal *Bilingualism: Language and Cognition*, *14*(1), 1–8.

Jarvis, S. (2016). Clarifying the scope of conceptual transfer. *Language Learning Journal*, *66*, 608–635.

Jarvis, S., & Pavlenko, A. (2008). *Crosslinguistic influence in language and cognition*. New York/London: Routledge.

Ji, Y., & Hohenstein, J. (2018). English and Chinese children's motion event similarity judgments. *Cognitive Linguistics*, *29*, 45–76.

Kaushanskaya, M., & Smith, S. (2016). Do grammatical–gender distinctions learned in the second language influence native-language lexical processing? *International Journal of Bilingualism, 20*(1), 30–39.

Kellerman, E., & van Hoof, A.-M. (2003). Manual accents. *International Review of Applied Linguistics, 41*, 251–269.

Kersten, A. W., Meissner, C. A., Lechuga, J. et al. (2010). English speakers attend more strongly than Spanish speakers to manner of motion when classifying novel objects and events. *Journal of Experimental Psychology: General, 139*(4), 638–653.

Kita, S., & Özyürek, A. (2003). What does cross-linguistic variation in semantic coordination of speech and gesture reveal?: Evidence for an interface representation of spatial thinking and speaking. *Journal of Memory and Language, 48*(1), 16–32.

Kousta, S. T., Vinson, D. P., & Vigliocco, G. (2008). Investigating linguistic relativity through bilingualism: The case of grammatical gender. *Journal of Experimental Psychology: Learning, Memory, and Cognition, 34*, 843–858.

Koster, D., & Cadierno, T. (2019). The effect of language on recognition memory in first language and second language speakers: The case of placement events. *International Journal of Bilingualism, 23*(2), 651–669.

Kroll, J. F., & Bialystok, E. (2013). Understanding the consequences of bilingualism for language processing and cognition. *Journal of Cognitive Psychology, 25*, 497–514.

Kurinski, E., Jambor, E., & Sera, M. D. (2016). Spanish grammatical gender: Its effects on categorization in native Hungarian speakers. *International Journal of Bilingualism, 20*(1), 76–93.

Kurinski, E., & Sera, M. D. (2011). Does learning Spanish grammatical gender change English-speaking adults' categorization of inanimate objects? *Bilingualism: Language and Cognition, 14*, 203–220.

Lai, V. T., & Boroditsky, L. (2013). The immediate and chronic influence of spatio temporal metaphors on the mental representations of time in English, Mandarin, and Mandarin-English speakers. *Frontiers in Psychology, 4*, 1–10.

Lai, V. T., Rodriguez, G. G., & Narasimhan, B. (2014). Thinking-for-speaking in early and late bilinguals. *Bilingualism: Language and Cognition, 17*(1), 139–152.

Lakoff, G. (1990). The invariance hypothesis: Is abstract reason based on image-schemas? *Cognitive Linguistics, 1*(1), 39–74.

Lakoff, G., & Johnson, M. (1980). Conceptual metaphor in everyday language. *The Journal of Philosophy, 77*(8), 453–486.

Langacker, R. W. (1987). *Foundations of cognitive grammar: Theoretical prerequisites* (Vol. 1). Stanford, Calif.: Stanford University Press.

Langacker, R. W. (2000). *Grammar and conceptualization*. Berlin: Walter de Gruyter.

Langacker, R. W. (2008). *Cognitive grammar: An introduction*. Oxford: Oxford University.

Lantolf, J. P., & Poehner, M. E. (2014). *Sociocultural theory and the pedagogical imperative in L2 education: Vygotskian praxis and the research/practice divide*. London: Routledge.

Larrañaga, P., Treffers-Daller, J., Tidball, F., & Ortega, M. C. G. (2012). L1 transfer in the acquisition of manner and path in Spanish by native speakers of English. *International Journal of Bilingualism, 16*(1), 117–138.

Laws, J., Attwood, A., & Treffers-Daller, J. (2021). Unlearning the boundary-crossing constraint: processing instruction and the acquisition of motion event construal. *International Review of Applied Linguistics in Language Teaching*. https://doi.org/10.1515/iral-2020-0147

Leavitt, J. (2010). *Linguistic relativities: Language diversity and modern thought*. Cambridge: Cambridge University Press.

Levinson, S. C. (2001). Covariation between spatial language and cognition. *In Language acquisition and conceptual development* (pp. 566–588). Cambridge: Cambridge University Press.

Levinson, S. C. (2003). S*pace in language and cognition: Explorations in cognitive diversity*. Cambridge: Cambridge University Press.

Li, W. (2018). Translanguaging as a practical theory of language. *Applied Linguistics, 39*(1), 9–30.

Liu, Y.-T. (2018). Linguistic relativity in L2 acquisition: Chinese-English bilinguals' reading of Chinese counterfactual statements. *Language and Linguistics, 19*(1), 117–155.

Lucy, J. A. (1992a). *Grammatical categories and cognition: A case study of the linguistic relativity hypothesis*. Cambridge: Cambridge University Press.

Lucy, J. A. (1992b). *Language diversity and thought: A reformulation of the linguistic relativity hypothesis*. Cambridge: Cambridge University Press.

Lucy, J. A. (1996). The scope of linguistic relativity: An analysis and review of empirical research. In J. J. Gumperz & S. C. Levinson (Eds.), *Rethinking linguistic relativity* (pp. 37–69). Cambridge: Cambridge University Press.

Lucy, J. A. (1997). Linguistic relativity. *Annual Review of Anthropology, 26*(1), 291–312.

Lucy, J. A. (2014). Methodological approaches in the study of linguistic relativity. In L. Filipović & M. Pütz. (Eds.), *Multilingual cognition and language use: Processing and typological perspectives* (pp. 17–44). Amsterdam: John Benjamins.

Lucy, J. A. (2016). Recent advances in the study of linguistic relativity in historical context: A critical assessment. *Language Learning, 66*(3), 487–515.

Lucy, J. A., & Gaskins, S. (2001). Grammatical categories and the development of classification preferences: a comparative approach. In M. Bowerman & S. Levinson (Eds.), *Language acquisition and conceptual development* (pp. 257–283). Cambridge: Cambridge University Press.

Lucy, J. A., & Gaskins, S. (2003). Interaction of language type and referent type in the development of nonverbal classification preferences. In D. Gentner & S. Goldin-Meadow (Eds.), *Language in mind: Advances in the study of language and thought* (pp. 465–492). Cambridge, MA: MIT Press.

Lupyan, G. (2012). Linguistically modulated perception and cognition: The label-feedback hypothesis. *Frontiers in Psychology, 3*, 54.

Lupyan, G. (2016). The centrality of language in human cognition. *Language Learning, 66*(3), 516–553.

Lupyan, G., & Clark, A. (2015). Words and the world: Predictive coding and the language-perception-cognition interface. *Current Directions in Psychological Science, 24*(4), 279–284.

Lupyan, G., Rakison, D., & McClelland, J. (2007). Language is not just for talking – Redundant labels facilitate learning of novel categories. *Psychological Science, 18*(12), 1077–1083.

Lupyan, G., & Ward, E. J. (2013). Language can boost otherwise unseen objects into visual awareness. *Proceedings of the National Academy of Sciences, 110*(35), 14196–14201.

Majid, A., Bowerman, M., Kita, S., Haun, D. B., & Levinson, S. C. (2004). Can language restructure cognition? The case for space. *Trends in Cognitive Sciences, 8*(3), 108–114.

Malt, B., Jobe, R. L., Li, P. et al. (2016). What constrains simultaneous mastery of first and second language word use? *International Journal of Bilingualism, 20*(6), 684–699.

Malt, B., Li, P., Pavlenko, A., Zhu, H., & Ameel, E. (2015). Bidirectional lexical interaction in late immersed Mandarin-English bilinguals. *Journal of Memory and Language, 82*, 86–104.

Malt, B., & Sloman, S. (2003). Linguistic diversity and object naming by nonnative speakers of English. B*ilingualism: Language and Cognition, 6*, 47–67.

Mayer, R. E. (2001). *Multimedia learning*. New York: Cambridge University Press.

McNeill, D. (Ed.). (2000). *Language and gesture (Vol. 2)*. Cambridge: Cambridge University Press.

McNeill, D. (1997). Growth points cross-linguistically. In J. Nuyts, & E, Peterson (Eds.), *Language and conceptualization* (pp.190–212). Cambridge: Cambridge University Press.

McNeill, D. (2001). Analogic/analytic representations and cross-linguistic differences in thinking for speaking. *Cognitive Linguistics, 11*, 43–60.

McNeill, D. (2005). *Gesture and thought*. Chicago: The University of Chicago Press.

McNeill, D., & Duncan, S. (2000). Growth points in thinking-for-speaking. In D. McNeill (Ed.), *Language and gesture* (pp. 141–161). Cambridge: Cambridge University Press.

Miles, L. K., Tan, L., Noble, G. D., et al. (2011). Can a mind have two time lines? Exploring space–time mapping in Mandarin and English speakers. *Psychonomic Bulletin & Review, 18*(3), 598–604.

Montero-Melis, G., & Bylund, E. (2017). Getting the ball rolling: the cross-linguistic conceptualization of caused motion. *Language and Cognition, 9*(3), 446–472.

Montero-Melis, G., Jaeger, T. F., & Bylund, E. (2016). Thinking is modulated by recent linguistic experience: Second language priming affects perceived event similarity. *Language Learning, 66*(3), 636–665.

Montero-Perez, M., Peters, E., & Desmet, P. (2018). Vocabulary learning through viewing video: The effect of two enhancement techniques. *Computer Assisted Language Learning, 31*, 1–26.

Montrul, S. (2005). Second language acquisition and first language loss in adult early bilinguals: Exploring some differences and similarities. *Second Language Research, 21*(3), 199–249.

Munnich, E., Landau, B., & Dosher, B. A. (2001). Spatial language and spatial representation: A cross-linguistic comparison. *Cognition, 81*(3), 171–208.

Muñoz, C. (2008). Age-related differences in foreign language learning. Revisiting the empirical evidence. *International Review of Applied Linguistics in Language Teaching, 46*(3), 197–220.

Muñoz C. (2016). *Age and the rate of foreign language learning*. Clevedon: Multilingual Matters.

Negueruela, E., Lantolf, J. P., Jordan, S. R., & Gelabert, J. (2004). The 'private function' of gesture in second language speaking activity: A study of motion verbs and gesturing in English and Spanish. *International Journal of Applied Linguistics, 14*(1), 113–147.

Nicoladis, E., Da Costa, N., & Foursha-Stevenson, C. (2016). Discourse relativity in Russian-English bilingual preschoolers' classification of objects by gender. *International Journal of Bilingualism, 20*(1), 17–29.

Nicoladis, E., & Foursha-Stevenson, C. (2012). Language and culture effects on gender classification of objects. *Journal of Cross-Cultural Psychology, 43*, 1095–1109.

Odlin, T. (1989). *Language transfer: cross-linguistic influence in language learning.* Cambridge: Cambridge University Press.

Ortega, L. (2014). *Understanding second language acquisition.* London: Routledge.

Orwell, G. (1949). *Nineteen eighty-four.* A novel. London: Secker & Warburg.

Özçalışkan, Ş. (2016). Do gestures follow speech in bilinguals' description of motion? *Bilingualism: Language and Cognition, 19*(3), 644–653.

Özyürek, A., Kita, S., Allen, S., Furman, R., & Brown, A. (2005). How does linguistic framing of events influence co-speech gestures?: Insights from crosslinguistic variations and similarities. *Gesture, 5*(1–2), 219–240.

Paivio, A. (2014). *Mind and its evolution: A dual coding theoretical approach.* New York: Psychology Press.

Pan, X., & Jared, D. (2021). Effects of Chinese word structure on object perception in Chinese–English bilinguals: Evidence from an ERP visual oddball paradigm. *Bilingualism: Language and Cognition, 24*(1), 111–123.

Panayiotou, A. (2004a). Bilingual emotions: The untranslatable self. *Estudios de Sociolinguistica 5*(1), 1–19.

Panayiotou, A. (2004b). Switching codes, switching code: Bilinguals' emotional responses to English and Greek. *Journal of Multilingual and Multicultural Development, 25*, 124–139.

Papafragou, A., Hulbert, J., & Trueswell, J. (2008). Does language guide event perception? Evidence from eye movements. *Cognition, 108*(1), 155–184.

Papafragou, A., Massey, C., & Gleitman, L. (2002). Shake, rattle, 'n' roll: The representation of motion in language and cognition. *Cognition, 84*(2), 189–219.

Park, H. I. (2020). How do Korean–English bilinguals speak and think about motion events? Evidence from verbal and non-verbal tasks. *Bilingualism: Language and Cognition, 23*(3), 483–499.

Park, H. I., & Ziegler, N. (2014). Cognitive shift in the bilingual mind: Spatial concepts in Korean–English bilinguals. *Bilingualism: Language and Cognition, 17*(2), 410–430.

Pavlenko, A. (2000). New approaches to concepts in bilingual memory. *Bilingualism: Language and Cognition, 3*(1), 1–4.

Pavlenko, A. (1999). New approaches to concepts in bilingual memory. *Bilingualism: Language and Cognition, 2*, 209–230.

Pavlenko, A. (2002a). Emotions and the body in Russian and English. *Pragmatics and Cognition, 10*(1), 207–241.

Pavlenko, A. (2002b). Bilingualism and emotions. *Multilingua, 21*(1), 45–78.

Pavlenko, A. (2003). Eyewitness memory in late bilinguals: Evidence for discursive relativity. *International Journal of Bilingualism, 7*(3), 257–281.

Pavlenko, A. (2004). L2 influence and L1 attrition in adult bilingualism. In M. Schmid, B. Köpke, M. Keijzer & L. Weilemar (Eds.), *First language attrition: Interdisciplinary perspectives on methodological issues* (pp. 47–59). Amsterdam: John Benjamins.

Pavlenko, A. (2005). Bilingualism and thought. In J. F. Kroll & A. M. B. de Groot (Eds.), *Handbook of bilingualism: Psycholinguistic approaches* (pp. 433–453). New York: Oxford University Press.

Pavlenko, A. (2011). Thinking and speaking in two languages: Overview of the field. In A. Pavlenko (Ed.), *Thinking and speaking in two languages* (pp. 237–257). Bristol: Multilingual Matters.

Pavlenko, A. (2014). *The bilingual mind: And what it tells us about language and thought.* Cambridge: Cambridge University Press.

Pavlenko, A. (2016). Whorf's lost argument: Multilingual awareness. *Language Learning, 66*(3), 581–607.

Pavlenko, A., Jarvis, S., Melnyk, S., & Sorokina, A. (2017). Communicative relevance: Color references in bilingual and trilingual speakers. *Bilingualism: Language and Cognition, 20*(4), 853–866.

Pavlenko, A., & Malt, B. C. (2011). Kitchen Russian: Cross-linguistic differences and first-language object naming by Russian-English bilinguals. *Bilingualism: Language and Cognition, 14*(1), 19–45.

Pavlenko, A., & Volynsky, M. (2015). Motion encoding in Russian and English: Moving beyond Talmy's typology. *Modern Language Journal, 99*(1), 32–48.

Peters, E., Heynen, E., & Puimège, E. (2016). Learning vocabulary through audiovisual input: The differential effect of L1 subtitles and captions. *System, 63*, 134–148.

Peyraube, A. (2006). Motion events in Chinese: Diachronic study of directional complements. In M. Hickmann & S. Robert (Eds.), *Space in languages: Linguistic systems and cognitive categories* (pp. 121–135). Philadelphia: Benjamins.

Pinker, S. (1994). *The language instinct: The new science of language and mind.* London: Penguin.

Pinker, S. (2007). *The stuff of thought: Language as a window into human nature.* New York: Penguim Books.

Regier, T., & Kay, P. (2009). Color categories are culturally diverse in cognition as well as in language. *Cultural Research, 39*, 56–71.

Reinders, H., & Ellis, R. (2009). The effects of two types of input on intake and the acquisition of implicit and explicit knowledge. In R. Eliis,

S. Loewen, C. Elder et al. (Eds.), *Implicit and explicit knowledge in second language learning, testing and teaching* (pp. 282–302). Bristol: Multilingual Matters.

Roberson, D. (2005). The categorical perception of colors and facial expressions: The effect of verbal interference. *Memory & Cognition, 28*(6), 977–986.

Roberson, D., & Davidoff, J. (2000). The categorical perception of colors and facial expressions: The effect of verbal interference. *Memory & Cognition, 28*(6), 977–986.

Roberson, D., Davies, I., & Davidoff, J. (2000). Color categories are not universal: replications and new evidence from a stone-age culture. *Journal of Experimental Psychology: General, 129*, 369–398.

Roberson, D., Pak, H., & Hanley, J. R. (2008). Categorical perception of colour in the left and right visual field is verbally mediated: Evidence from Korean. *Cognition, 107*(2), 752–762.

Rodgers, M. P. H., & Webb, S. (2017). The effects of captions on EFL learners' comprehension of English-Language television programs. *CALICO Journal, 34*, 20–38.

Sachs, O., & Coley, J. (2006). Envy and jealousy in Russian and English: Labeling and conceptualization of emotions by monolinguals and bilinguals: Emotional experience, expression, and representation. In A. Pavlenko (Ed.), *Bilingual minds: emotional experience, expression, and representation* (pp. 209–231). Clevedon: Multilingual Matters.

Samuelson, L. K. (2002). Statistical regularities in vocabulary guide language acquisition in connectionist models and 15–20-month-olds. *Developmental Psychology, 38*(6), 1016–1037.

Samuel, S., Cole, G., & Eacott, M. J. (2019). Grammatical gender and linguistic relativity: A systematic review. *Psychonomic Bulletin & Review, 26*(6), 1767–1786.

Sato, S., & Athanasopoulos, P. (2018). Grammatical gender affects gender perception: Evidence for the structural-feedback hypothesis. *Cognition, 176*, 220–231.

Sato, S., Casaponsa, A., & Athanasopoulos, P. (2020). Flexing gender perception: Brain potentials reveal the cognitive permeability of grammatical information. *Cognitive Science, 44*(9), e12884.

Sato, S., Gygax, P. M., & Gabriel, U. (2013). Gender inferences: Grammatical features and their impact on the representation of gender in bilinguals. *Bilingualism: Language and Cognition, 16*(4), 792–807.

Schmid, M. S. (2011). *Language Attrition*. Cambridge: Cambridge University Press.

Sidnell, J., & Enfield, N. (2012). Language diversity and social action: A third locus of linguistic relativity. *Current Anthropology, 53*(3), 302–333.

Slobin, D. I. (1987). Thinking for speaking. Proceedings of the annual meeting of the Berkeley. *Linguistic Society, 13,* 435–445.

Slobin, D. I. (1991). Learning to think for speaking: Native language, cognition and rhetorical style. *Pragmatics, 1*(1), 7–29.

Slobin, D. I. (1996). From 'thought and language' to 'thinking for speaking'. In J. Gumperz & S. Levinson (Eds.), *Rethinking linguistic relativity* (pp. 70–96). Cambridge: Cambridge University Press.

Slobin, D. I. (2000). Verbalised events: A dynamic approach to linguistic relativity and determinism. In S. Niemeier. & R. Dirven. (Eds.), *Evidence for linguistic relativity* (pp. 107–138). Amsterdam, The Netherlands: John Benjamins.

Slobin, D. I. (2003). Language and thought online: Cognitive consequences of linguistic relativity. In D. Gentner & S. Goldin-Meadow (Eds.), *Language in mind: Advances in the study of language and thought* (pp. 157–192). Cambridge, MA: MIT Press.

Slobin, D. I. (2006). What makes manner of motion salient? Explorations in linguistic typology, discourse, and cognition. In M. Hickmann & S. Robert (Eds.), *Space in languages: Linguistic systems and cognitive categories* (pp. 59–81). Amsterdam & Philadelphia: John Benjamins.

Slobin, D. I., & Hoiting, N. (1994). Reference to movement in spoken and signed languages: Typological considerations. In *Annual Meeting of the Berkeley Linguistics Society, 20* (1), 487–505.

Smith, L. B. (2010). *Learning how to learn words: An associative crane.* New York: Oxford University Press.

Smith, L. B., & Samuelson, L. (2006). An attentional learning account of the shape bias: Reply to Cimpian and Markman (2005) and Booth, Waxman, and Huang (2005). *Developmental Psychology, 42*(6), 1339–1343.

So, W. C. (2010). Cross-cultural transfer in gesture frequency in Chinese-English bilinguals. *Language and Cognitive Processes, 25,* 1335–1353.

Stam, G. (2006). Thinking for speaking about motion: L1 and L2 speech and gesture. *International Review of Applied Linguistics, 44,* 143–169.

Stam, G. (2010). Can an L2 speaker's patterns of thinking for speaking change?. In Z. Han & T. Cadierno (Eds.), *Linguistic relativity in SLA: Thinking for speaking* (pp. 59–83). Bristol: Multilingual Matters.

Stam, G. (2015). Changes in thinking for speaking: A longitudinal case study. *The Modern Language Journal, 99*(S1), 83–99.

Stam, G., Lantolf, J., Urbanski, K., & Smotrova, T. (2021, April 16–17). *How concept-based instruction works in teaching and thinking for speaking in an L2*

[Paper presentation]. Can Motion Event Construal be Taught or Restructured? Evidence from Bilinguals and L2 Learners, Reading, UK.

Stocker, L., & Berthele, R. (2020). The roles of language mode and dominance in French-German bilinguals' motion event descriptions. *Bilingualism: Language and Cognition, 23*(3), 519–531.

Syodorenko, T. (2010). Modality of input and vocabulary acquisition. *Language Learning & Technology, 14*(2), 50–73.

Talmy, L. (1985). Lexicalization patterns: Semantic structure in lexical forms. In T. Shopen (Ed.), *Grammatical categories and the lexicon. Language typology syntactic description* (Vol. 3, pp. 57–149). Cambridge: Cambridge University Press.

Talmy, L. (2000). *Toward a cognitive semantics*. Cambridge: MIT Press.

Tang, M., Vanek, N., & Roberts, L. (2021). Crosslinguistic influence on English and Chinese L2 speakers' conceptualization of event series. *International Journal of Bilingualism, 25*(1), 205–223.

Thierry, G. (2016). Neurolinguistic relativity: How language flexes human perception and cognition. *Language Learning, 66*(3), 690–713.

Thierry, G., Athanasopoulos, P., Wiggett, A., Dering, B., & Kuipers, J. (2009). Unconscious effects of language-specific terminology on pre-attentive color perception. *Proceedings of the National Academy of Sciences, 106*, 4567–4570.

Thierry, G., & Wu, Y. J. (2007). Brain potentials reveal unconscious translation during foreign-language comprehension. *Proceedings of the National Academy of Sciences, 104*(30), 12530–12535.

Tokowicz, N., Michael, E. B., & Kroll, J. F. (2004). The roles of study-abroad experience and working-memory capacity in the types of errors made during translation. *Bilingualism: Language and Cognition, 7*(3), 255–272.

Tomczak, E., & Ewert, A. (2015). Real and fictive motion processing in Polish L2 users of English and monolinguals: Evidence for different conceptual representations. *The Modern Language Journal, 99*(S1), 49–65.

Treffers-Daller, J. (2016). Language dominance: The construct, its measurement, and operationalization. In C. Silva-Corvalán & J. Treffers-Daller (Eds.), *Language dominance in bilinguals: Issues of measurement and operationalization* (pp. 235–265). Cambridge: Cambridge University Press.

Treffers-Daller, J., & Calude, A. (2015). The role of statistical learning in the acquisition of motion event construal in a second language. *International Journal of Bilingual Education and Bilingualism, 18*(5), 602–623.

Treffers-Daller, J., & Tidball, F. (2015). Can L2 learners learn new ways to conceptualise events? Evidence from motion event construal among English-speaking learners of French. In P. Guijarro-Fuentes, K. Schmitz & N. Müller

(Eds.), *The acquisition of French in multi-lingual contexts* (pp. 145–184). Bristol: Multilingual Matters.

Trueswell, J. C., & Papafragou, A. (2010). Perceiving and remembering event cross-linguistically: Evidence from dual-task paradigms. *Journal of Memory and Language, 63*(1), 64–82.

Tyler, A. (2012). *Cognitive linguistics and second language learning: Theoretical basics and experimental evidence.* New York/London: Routledge.

Vanderplank, R. (2010). Déjà vu? A decade of research on language laboratories, television and video in language learning. *Language Teaching, 43*(1), 1–37.

Vanek, N. (2020). Changing event categorization in second language users through perceptual learning. *Language Learning, 70*(2), 309–348.

Vanek, N., & Hendriks, H. (2015). Convergence of temporal reference frames in sequential bilinguals: Event structuring unique to second language users. *Bilingualism: Language and Cognition, 18*(4), 753–768.

Vanek, N., & Selinker, L. (2017). Covariation between temporal interlanguage features and nonverbal event categorisation. *International Review of Applied Linguistics in Language Teaching, 55*(3), 223–243.

VanPatten, B. (2004). *Processing instruction: Theory, research, and commentary.* Mahwah: Erlbaum.

VanPatten, B. (2015). Foundations of processing instruction. *International Review of Applied Linguistics in Language Teaching, 53*(2), 91–109.

VanPatten, B., & Benati, A. (2010). *Key terms in second language acquisition.* London: Bloomsbury.

VanPatten, B., & Cadierno, T. (1993). Explicit instruction and input processing. *Studies in Second Language Acquisition, 15*(2), 225–243.

von Humboldt, W. (1963). *Humanist without portfolio: An anthology of the writings of Wilhelm von Humboldt.* Detroit, MI: Wayne State University Press.

von Stutterheim, C., Andermann, M., Carroll, M., Flecken, M., & Schmiedtova, B. (2012). How grammaticized concepts shape event conceptualization in language production: Insights from linguistic analysis, eye tracking data, and memory performance. *Linguistics, 50*(4), 833–867.

von Stutterheim, C., Bouhaous, A., & Carroll, M. (2017). From time to space: The impact of aspectual categories on the construal of motion events: The case of Tunisian Arabic and Modern Standard Arabic. *Linguistics, 55*(1), 207–249.

von Stutterheim, C. & Carroll, M. (2006). The impact of grammatical temporal categories on ultimate attainment in L2 learning. In H. Byrnes, H. Weger-Guntharp & K. Sprang. (Eds.), *Educating for advanced foreign language capacities* (pp. 40–53). Georgetown: Georgetown University Press.

von Stutterheim, C., & Nuse, R. (2003). Processes of conceptualization in language production: language-specific perspectives and event construal. *Linguistics, 41*(5), 851–881.

Vygotsky, L. S. (2012). *Thought and language*. Cambridge/London: MIT press.

Wang, Y. (2020). *Cognitive restructuring in the multilingual mind: motion event construal in Cantonese-English-Japanese multilingual speakers* (Doctoral dissertation, UCL (University College London)).

Wang, Y., & Li, W. (2019). Cognitive restructuring in the bilingual mind: Motion event construal in early Cantonese-English bilinguals. *Language and Cognition*, *11*(4), 527–554.

Wang, Y., & Li, W. (2021a). Cognitive restructuring in the multilingual mind: language-specific effects on processing efficiency of caused motion events in Cantonese–English–Japanese speakers. *Bilingualism: Language and Cognition*, *24*(4), 730–745.

Wang, Y., & Li, W. (2021b). Two languages, one mind: the effects of language learning on motion event processing in early Cantonese-English bilinguals. *Proceedings of the Annual Meeting of the Cognitive Science Society*, *43*(43), 2169–2175.

Wang, Y., & Li, W. (2022). Multilingual learning and cognitive restructuring: The role of audiovisual media exposure in Cantonese-English-Japanese multilinguals' motion event cognition. *International Journal of Bilingualism*. https://doi.org/10.1177/13670069221085565

Whorf, B. L. (1940/1956). Linguistics as an exact science. *Technology Review*, 43, 61–63, 80–83. Reprinted in J. B. Carroll (Ed.), *Language, thought, and reality: Selected writings of Benjamin Lee Whorf* (pp. 220–232). Cambridge, MA: MIT Press.

Whorf, B. L. (1956). *Language, thought, and reality*. Cambridge, MA: MIT Press.

Winawer, J., Nathan, W., Michael, C. F. et al. (2007). Russian blues reveal effects of language on color discrimination. *Proceedings of the National Academy of Sciences*, *104*(19), 7780–7785.

Wolff, P., & Holmes, K. J. (2011). Linguistic relativity. Wiley interdisciplinary reviews: *Cognitive Science*, *2*(3), 253–265.

Wolff, P., & Malt, B. C. (2010). The language-thought interface: an Introduction. In P. Wolff & B. C. Malt (Eds.), *Words and the mind: How words capture human experience* (pp. 3–15). Oxford: Oxford University Press.

Yoshida, H., & Smith, L. B. (2001). Early noun lexicons in English and Japanese. *Cognition*, *82*, B63–B74.

Yoshida, H., & Smith, L. B. (2003). Known and novel noun extensions: Attention at two levels of abstraction. *Child Development*, *74*, 564–577.

Zhang, H., & Vanek, N. (2021). From 'No, she does' to 'Yes, she does': Negation processing in negative yes–no questions by Mandarin speakers of English. *Applied Psycholinguistics*, *42*(4), 937–967.

Cambridge Elements ☰

Second Language Acquisition

Alessandro Benati

The University of Hong Kong

Alessandro Benati is Director of CAES at The University of Hong Kong (HKU). He is known for his work in second language acquisition and second language teaching. He has published groundbreaking research on the pedagogical framework called Processing Instruction. He is co-editor of a new online series for Cambridge University Press, a member of the REF Panel 2021, and Honorary Professor at York St John University.

John W. Schwieter

Wilfrid Laurier University, Ontario

John W. Schwieter is Associate Professor of Spanish and Linguistics, and Faculty of Arts Teaching Scholar, at Wilfrid Laurier University. His research interests include psycholinguistic and neurolinguistic approaches to multilingualism and language acquisition; second language teaching and learning; translation and cognition and language, culture and society.

About the Series

Second Language Acquisition showcases a high-quality set of updatable, concise works that address how learners come to internalize the linguistic system of another language and how they make use of that linguistic system. Contributions reflect the interdisciplinary nature of the field, drawing on theories, hypotheses and frameworks from education, linguistics, psychology and neurology, among other disciplines. Each Element in this series addresses several important questions: What are the key concepts?; What are the main branches of research?; What are the implications for SLA?; What are the implications for pedagogy?; What are the new avenues for research? and What are the key readings?.

Cambridge Elements ☰

Second Language Acquisition

Printed in the United States
by Baker & Taylor Publisher Services

Printed in the United States
by Baker & Taylor Publisher Services